Recent Themes in the History of Africa and the Atlantic World

Historians in Conversation:
Recent Themes in Understanding the Past
Series editor, Louis A. Ferleger

Recent Themes in

THE HISTORY OF AFRICA AND THE ATLANTIC WORLD

Historians in Conversation

Edited by Donald A. Yerxa

THE UNIVERSITY OF SOUTH CAROLINA PRESS

Published by the University of South Carolina Press
Columbia, South Carolina 29208

www.sc.edu/uscpress

Manufactured in the United States of America

17 16 15 14 13 12 11 10 09 08   10 9 8 7 6 5 4 3 2 1

Library of Congress Cataloging-in-Publication Data

Recent themes in the history of Africa and the Atlantic world : historians in conversation /
    edited by Donald A. Yerxa.
        p. cm. — (Historians in conversation)
    A collection of essays, forums, and interviews originally appearing in Historically speaking.
    Includes bibliographical references and index.
    ISBN 978-1-57003-757-3 (cloth : alk. paper) — ISBN 978-1-57003-758-0 (pbk : alk.
paper)
    1. Africa—Historiography. 2. Atlantic Ocean Region—Historiography. 3. Equiano,
Olaudah, b. 1745– —Historiography. I. Yerxa, Donald A., 1950– II. Historically speaking.
    DT19.R38 2008
    960.072—dc22

                                                                        2008008026

Contents

PART 2. THE ATLANTIC WORLD

Series Editor's Preface

The Historical Society was founded in 1997 to create more venues for common conversations about the past. Consequently, in the autumn of 2001, the Historical Society launched a new type of publication. The society's president, George Huppert, and I believed that there was an important niche for a publication that would make the work of the most prominent historians more accessible to nonspecialists and general readers. We recruited two historians who shared this vision, Joseph S. Lucas and Donald A. Yerxa, and asked them to transform *Historically Speaking* into a journal of historical ideas. Up to that point, *Historically Speaking* had served as an in-house publication reporting on the society's activities and its members' professional accomplishments. Yerxa and Lucas quickly changed the layout and content of *Historically Speaking,* and within a short period of time many of the most prominent historians in the world began appearing in its pages—people such as Danielle Allen, Niall Ferguson, Daniel Walker Howe, Mary Lefkowitz, Pauline Maier, William McNeill, Geoffrey Parker, and Sanjay Subrahmanyam. *Historically Speaking*'s essays, forums, and interviews have drawn widespread attention. *The Chronicle of Higher Education*'s "Magazine and Journal Reader" section, for example, repeatedly has highlighted pieces appearing in *Historically Speaking.* And leading historians are loyal readers, praising *Historically Speaking* as a "must-read" journal, a "*New York Review of Books* for history," and "the most intellectually exciting publication in history that is currently available."

The Historical Society is pleased to partner with the University of South Carolina Press to publish a multivolume series, Historians in Conversation: Recent Themes in Understanding the Past. Each thematic volume pulls key essays, forums, and interviews from *Historically Speaking* and makes them accessible for classroom use and for the general reader. The original selections from *Historically Speaking* are supplemented with an introductory essay by Donald A. Yerxa along with suggestions for further reading.

We welcome your interest in the Historical Society. You may find us on the Internet at www.bu.edu/historic. You may also contact us at the Historical Society, 656 Beacon St., Mezzanine, Boston, Mass., 02215-2010, telephone 617-358-0260.

LOUIS A. FERLEGER

Acknowledgments

The volumes in this series are utterly dependent on the willingness of superb scholars to share their insights with others, especially nonspecialists. The contributors to this volume on Africa and the Atlantic world eased the several editorial tasks considerably, and I am keenly grateful to all of them. I am especially appreciative of Joseph Miller's support and encouragement of this and other projects.

Recent Themes in the History of Africa and the Atlantic World—as well as every issue of *Historically Speaking*—reflects the many talents of Joseph Lucas and Randall Stephens, two extremely gifted historian-editors who help make my job both a pleasure and an intellectual adventure. And I am indebted to Bill Adams and the fine editorial staff of the University of South Carolina Press for their valuable assistance at every turn.

Introduction

Coherence, Complexity, and the Place of Africa and the Atlantic World in World History

Donald A. Yerxa

"**P**erhaps in the future there will be some African history to teach. But at present there is none, or very little: there is only the history of Europe in Africa."[1] Dismissive remarks like these made in 1963 by the late Hugh Trevor-Roper would be unthinkable today. African history is a well-established field, and in the decades since Trevor-Roper's unfortunate comment, an avalanche of scholarship has illuminated the African past. That said, questions remain about how adequately the history of Africa is being integrated into world history. And when the attempt is made, does the African past get flattened out, as Patrick Manning notes, with single, civilization-wide generalizations?[2]

The November/December 2004 issue of *Historically Speaking* addressed the important question of Africa's place in world history at multiple levels. The genesis of this conversation was a session at the 2003 meeting of the African Studies Association where some Africanists and world historians discussed how better to integrate Africa into world history narratives. Opinions ranged from outright skepticism that world historians can refrain from resorting to clichés that homogenize and distort the rich complexity of the African past to criticism of Africanists for failing to supply world historians with provisional generalizations gleaned from several decades of specialized scholarship. Such concerns are fairly typical in historical conversations these days. Many fields of history struggle to find a healthy balance between specialized inquiries that focus on the particular and the local and the search for larger patterns that bring coherence to our understanding of the past.[3] Complexity and coherence are not sworn enemies, but they can be uneasy bedfellows at times.

Beyond these predictable concerns, however, lies another set of questions to ponder, and prominent Africanist historian Joseph C. Miller is raising them. Is it legitimate, for example, to interpret African history on the basis of modern Western conceptual schemes and historiographical conventions? And how can historians produce more satisfactory transregional accounts that interpret the Atlantic, Mediterranean, or Indian Ocean experiences as much from African premises as from familiar Western ones? Such questions contain assumptions and carry implications that challenge how we conceptualize historical inquiry today. We reprint in this volume Miller's provocative think piece and a number of responses to it, followed by a rejoinder.

Miller argues that historians should incorporate multiple perspectives when doing world history. He makes the case that Africa must be brought into world history "on Africans' terms." If Africa enters world history based only on European or Asian standards (e.g., civilization orientation), we repeat Trevor-Roper's error and hold the African past in intellectual bondage. So a truly multicentric approach is needed. The exchange is very telling. It shows how leading historians are grappling with the important conceptual matters at this particular stage in the world history project. With that in mind, it is also interesting to note Manning's observation that while multicentrism is no doubt the best way to write world history at this juncture, doing so adds further complexity that "threatens cacophony." Again that tension between coherence and complexity.

While historians debate Africa's proper place in world history, there is no doubting the significance of West Africa in the maturing field of Atlantic history. This promising and popular field is not easy to define, however, because the dominant characteristics of Atlantic history shift over time. Bernard Bailyn, one of its most prominent practitioners, warns against viewing the Atlantic world as a static historical unit. Atlantic history is not simply "the aggregate of four or five discrete European histories together with the regional histories of the native peoples of West Africa and America." It is, Bailyn argues, more than the sum of its parts.[4] In his assessment of Atlantic history included in this volume, Trevor Burnard offers two succinct descriptions of the field—one that the historian-geographer D. W. Meinig wrote over twenty years ago, the other Burnard's own formulation. Meinig spoke of "a sudden and harsh encounter between two old worlds that transformed both and integrated them into a single New World."[5] For Burnard the principal theme of Atlantic history is that from the fifteenth century to the present, the Atlantic world was "not just a physical fact [or a geographic expression] but a particular zone of exchange and interchange, circulation, and transmission."[6]

Once again we are confronted with the tension between coherence and complexity. In his 1981 American Historical Association presidential address Bailyn concluded that the greatest challenge historians then faced was "how to put the story together again" without sacrificing the rich complexity that specialized scholarship was revealing.[7] At one level, Atlantic history represents a response to the challenge of fragmentation brought on by the proliferation of specialized subfields of historical investigation. Echoing Bailyn, Burnard suggests that Atlantic history "offers historians an escape from the self-defeating tendency to study smaller and smaller units unconnected with larger processes." But, as Burnard also notes, not all Atlanticists are as concerned as Bailyn about the lack of coherence in historical scholarship today. Indeed many "celebrate marginality rather than integration and focus on disaggregation as much as aggregation."[8]

One of the icons of Atlantic history is the ex-slave, Olaudah Equiano (renamed Gustavus Vassa by a Royal Navy officer). Equiano's *Interesting Narrative of the Life of Olaudah Equiano, or Gustavus Vassa the African. Written by Himself* (London, 1789) is widely used in college classrooms to acquaint students with the horrors of the transatlantic Middle Passage as well as with life in eighteenth-century West Africa. According to Vincent Carretta, Equiano was a true man of the Atlantic, "a central figure in the reconstruction of Atlantic history, and to our understanding of the Atlantic world." But what if Equiano was actually born in South Carolina and had fabricated his African identity? Carretta contends that this may well have been the case, but the important point about Equiano was that he was indeed "an Atlantic creole" (Ira Berlin's phrase) whose life and writings in many ways demonstrate the realities of the Atlantic world.[9] Not everyone agrees with Carretta on whether Equiano lied about his identity or, if he did, how much that matters. We include a spirited forum on this question in this volume. And, once again, we catch a glimpse of a fundamental challenge historians face today: constructing narratives that give coherence to a messy and complex past without sacrificing its richness and texture.

NOTES

1. Hugh Trevor-Roper, "The Rise of Christian Europe," *Listener,* November 28, 1963, 5.

2. Patrick Manning, "Africa in World History and Historiography," *Historically Speaking* 6 (November/December 2004): 15.

3. See John Hedley Brooke, "Science, Religion, and Historical Complexity," *Historically Speaking* 8 (May/June 2007): 10–13; Donald A. Yerxa, "Historical

Coherence, Complexity, and the Scientific Revolution," *European Review* 15 (October 2007): 439–44.

4. Bernard Bailyn, *Atlantic History: Concept and Contours* (Cambridge, Mass.: Harvard University Press, 2005), 60.

5. D. W. Meinig, *The Shaping of America: A Geographical Perspective on 500 Years of History* (New Haven, Conn.: Yale University Press, 1986), 65. Quoted in Bailyn, *Atlantic History,* 55–56.

6. Trevor Burnard, "Only Connect: The Rise and Rise (and Fall?) of Atlantic History," *Historically Speaking* 7 (July/August 2006): 20.

7. Bernard Bailyn, "The Challenge of Modern Historiography," *American Historical Review* 87 (February 1982): 23–24.

8. Burnard, "Only Connect," 20.

9. Vincent Carretta, "Does Equiano Still Matter?" *Historically Speaking* 7 (January/February 2006): 2–7.

PART 1

Africa and World History

Beyond Blacks, Bondage, and Blame

Why a Multicentric World History Needs Africa

Joseph C. Miller

As Lauren Benton put it recently, "World history has not produced a significant volume of methodologically thoughtful discussions or theoretically influential studies."[1] As a historian, I have to agree. As an Africanist, I have long thought that the particular "peoples without history" whom I contemplate offer the extreme examples of the exclusion that conventional untheorized standards of world history impose—less and more implicitly—on most of the world. Most world historians—with respect but not apologies to my many friends who thus style themselves—seem also to mute, if not negate, central principles of history's distinctive methodology. Those who adhere to a "civilizational" approach isolate the exceptional by relying on "continuity" and "origins" in ways that neglect history's core emphasis on change arising from contingency and complexity. Those who isolate single "causes"—or even several "causes"—of change violate history's distinctive reasoning from contexts, the particulars of time and place.

It is not that world historians have not made gains: only that they have reached the limits of gains achievable within the framework of an essentially nationalist, particularist, exclusive, and progressive epistemology. In fact, Africans (like the vast majority of the world's people) have had, and have, distinctive ways of thinking about themselves and their world(s), as well as about the greater world they share with us. These are worth knowing, not just for their abstract value as human creations but also for the very practical and revealing highlights that their alternatives cast on the modern Western imaginings that make up our reality.

From *Historically Speaking* 6 (November/December 2004)

The first generation of trained historians interested in Africa—Edward Blyden and others in Africa, and W. E. B. Du Bois, Leo Hansberry, and colleagues of African descent in the United States, trained before the First World War—played by European rules. They concentrated on the earliest, largest, most powerful, monument-building "states" in Africa that they could identify. Their identification of pharaonic Egypt (third to first millennium B.C.E.), or at least Nubia, as "African," their delineation of "empires" in the sub-Saharan western *sudan* (tenth to sixteenth centuries C.E.), and their admiration for the mysterious monumental stone ruins in southeastern Africa at Great Zimbabwe (thirteenth to fourteenth centuries C.E.) survive today as the touchstones of most world history references to Africa before the fateful era of the Atlantic slave trade. King Tut preceded Alexander and Augustus, and Mansa Musa of Mali (ca. 1320s) reigned before Elizabeth I or Phillip II.

For most, this progressive vision of Africa's past presents gripping achievements, farseeing paradigms for modernity, and all the more poignantly because these "black" achievers constructed them in defiance of hostile modern racial stereotypes. The story is tragic because later Africans, unlike Europeans, seemingly lost the opportunity to build on such promising foundations. Of course, all of this evidence of ancient African accomplishment appeals to modern liberals concerned to move beyond the racial divisions under which we still labor. It is a narrative ready-made for introducing Africa respectably into a global history for youthful beginners barely aware of the world beyond their personal, very contemporary, and only hazily (even) national experiences. But it thereby also trades on (by playing off) precisely the modern, often implicitly racial, distortions that exclude Africa from a history of the world that might include Africans' own visions of struggle and accomplishment.

Within the mainstream academy, scholars first sought these distinctively African perspectives not through history but rather through anthropology, a discipline distinguished from the several academic disciplines on which it drew only by its focus on "Others." Anthropology appealed to liberals because it substituted nonbiological (and hence value neutral in an age that believed in biology as destiny) distinctions in learned, hence alterable, social and cultural practice (in a progressive age that also believed in social engineering) for the prejudicial biological ranking of human differentiation that underlay the racism of colonial times. But the difference on which anthropology thrived still rested on the premise that Others were exotic; the anthropologist assumed the heroic role of penetrating the superficial unintelligibility of what Others did to reveal the (implicitly surprising) "rationality of natives"[2]

—reason construed variously as "culture," "structure," "function," and so on. The trouble was that the "rationality of natives" turned out to lie, once again, largely in the mind of the ethnographic observer. Early to mid-twentieth-century anthropology was thus no less a child of European modernity than was history, and it similarly selected what made sense to Westerners from whatever else that might have been discerned "out there" among the Rest.

For outsiders to African history, the reigning anthropological derivative has been the "tribe." Today people in Africa may use the term to claim "tribal" political affiliations, but applied to the past the word retains the quasi-racist connotations of "primitive" that it acquired in colonial times. As a result, today's historians of Africa have banished the word *tribe* from their vocabulary. But even polite (if not politically correct) Africanist speech retains a tendency to recognize Africans principally by the company they keep, under elaborately respectful euphemisms—"ethnic" or "linguistic" or "ethno-linguistic."

The laudable quest to render Africans respectable by comfortable, familiar standards—whether as builders of states and monuments or as members of ethnicized cultures—thus inevitably excludes nearly all the ideas and strategies important to people in Africa, precisely because the forms in which Africans' ideas became familiar to outsiders were the ones that Europeans constructed to render Africans incompetent, if not also contrastingly repugnant. They are the specific components of the "blackness" and "bondage" under which (undifferentiated) "Africans" still labor in much world history.

As the title of these remarks implies, I think that historians of Africa are now prepared to offer a superior alternative that makes such union of Africa and history not only possible but also necessary for the integrity of both. But to do so they must step beyond modern preoccupations—mostly derived from values like individual freedom and the political tensions of race—that continue to exclude Africa from a viable role in a balanced, multicentric world history of complexity. Given the racial politics of history in Africa, there is an urgency about doing it right, not only doing right by people in Africa (and by their descendants in the diaspora who claim its heritage as their own) but also moving historical epistemology beyond its preoccupation with triumphal progress and toward the more ironic, even tragic, story of all humanity.

Philosophers of African thought have long insisted on Africa's communal ethos: individuals "existed" not because they could think, alone, for themselves (a notion predicated on a sense of a stable self, generated internally, independently of context—*pace* Descartes, who marked the threshold of

European modernity in precisely these terms) but rather because they affiliated themselves with consummate flexibility with others around them: "I am, because I *belong*"; or, "I am because we are."[3] On that philosophical basis, identity is relative, a fluid social and contextual sensibility, and Africans worked out multiple identities to seek success through flexible strategies of accumulating connections, of constructing social contexts rather than taking them as given.

People in Africa, rather than emphasizing technologies of appropriating nonhuman sources of energy, sought productivity (and power) by controlling the efforts of the people around them, through multiple distinctions of age, gender, rank, among other means of differentiation—increasingly, after 1700 or so, including slavery. The multiplicity of identities multiplied the systems of ranking, in a kind of inflationary process that gave more people more means of claiming superiority over others in one defined context or another, however they might simultaneously be outranked on other spectra they did not control. So much for the validity of reducing Africans' identities to single-dimensional "ethnicities" and particularly inherited or determining ones. Following this African logic, one ends up conceptualizing power as an abstract externality that individuals accessed or asserted rather than something inherent in individuals themselves. One also senses the naive simplicity of the single-dimensional notion of rank and power that emerges from modern individualism, which cannot encompass the fundamentally competitive strategies of "belonging" that motivated action, and hence history, in Africa.

To extend this kind of contrast to those familiar "ancient African kingdoms" and "empires" that conventionally enter less multicentric versions of world history, I turn to pharaonic Egypt, Nubia, the "empires" in the sub-Saharan western *sudan,* and the mysterious but monumental stone ruins at Great Zimbabwe in southeastern Africa. The flexibility and multiplicity of identity in Africa rendered irrelevant most of such progressivist history (or the equivalent Weberian political sociology) that structures modern (nation-) state–centered global histories in terms of modern political and military power. But Africans in fact thought of political community not as institutionalized collectivities of this sort but rather in terms of ongoing, direct, face-to-face negotiations. Politics was a dynamic process of personal interaction rather than relationships stabilized by "hegemony" or "legitimacy" or any of the other modern fictions necessary to explain "structures" that work by abstraction rather than through continuous, real-time confrontation and collaboration.

Historians of medieval Europe now rightly distinguish chivalric politics there from early modern "absolute" monarchies (never mind modern state

systems) and construct their political histories around the long series of circumstantial, incremental steps through which Europeans struggled with one
another to construct the latter out of the former. Political history in Mali or
Songhai was no less conflict-ridden and dynamic and merits similar respect.
It is not the essentially static imaginings of modern Europeans of these as
"states" that historians ought to incorporate into their global narratives but
instead the human dilemmas of power, the many different strategies that people invented to work their ways out of specific contradictions.

The process of how closed domestic communities engage the openness of
commercial economies leads directly to the sensitive issue of African involvement in Atlantic slaving. If one starts from the evident premise that in Africa
one succeeded in the highly competitive personal and communal environments that I've described by aggregating followings of people—by taking
wives and enlisting clients, siring children, and acquiring vulnerable strangers
as dependents—then we shift our focus from who *sold* whom to Europeans
to how *buyers* in Africa deployed the textiles, currencies, alcohol, and guns
that they acquired from the Atlantic to assemble the large personal followings
on the most dependent terms they could impose: that is, especially (but not
only) including the uprooted, isolated, and hence vulnerable strangers whom
we would describe as "slaves." Powerful Africans accordingly distinguished
dependents they acquired for sale from others whom they meant to keep. The
competitiveness of this process, as in the modern international arms race,
meant that some survived only by escalating the struggle to the level of violence. The result in Africa paralleled what political economists have characterized in Europe as a violent phase of "primitive accumulation" at the
threshold of the individuation of property and identity on which modern
capitalism later rose.

African warlords assembled vulnerable refugees and structured them in
coherent groups for self-defense. Military leaders gained unprecedented political power over these refugees initially in return for protecting them from
other warlords. Some warlords captured still others to keep and employ as
agents of their personal power or to sell for still more imports with which
they could buy the loyalties of subjects growing reluctant or resentful at the
costs of defense. They thus created the (mostly) eighteenth-century "states"
of the Atlantic coastal regions (though the processes I am describing are
meant to accent these as highly dynamic entities, anything but static
"states"). Further recruitment through slaving eventually allowed other entrepreneurs to convert commercial opportunity into increased human in-
vestment in production and greater (human) productivity in an economic

process of "development" that sustained Africa's growing exchanges with the growing Atlantic economy.

On the scale of world history, these dispersed, continentally specific strategies of seizing local resources were realizations of a single pan-Atlantic (and ultimately global) integrative economic process. Phrased in this differentially inclusive way, it becomes clear that people in Africa participated no less than anyone else but in the distinctive ways—conceptually, economically, environmentally—accessible to them under the pressures of the accelerating pace of change that capitalist strategies enabled. In Africa these engagements —first Asian, then Muslim, and only belatedly Christian—went back at least to the eighth century. By the eighteenth century Europeans were culpable in the sense of being "enablers" who provided the commercial credit (more important than the guns). But the issues for Africans, and the only bases for understanding their active engagement in the exchange, were their own. World historical processes are generated through—and because of—the specific and differing ways in which people experience them.

That's the European version of the story, told in political and economic terms that you may regard as familiar, even trivial, however much they may convey some sense of novelty when applied to Africa. Working my way a bit farther out on my limb, I'll propose that "witchcraft" (NB: *our* designation of the experience) provided the terms in which most people in Africa experienced the human exploitation of this era. But we must suspend our modern prejudice against our own distorted notion of "witchcraft" only as "superstition" to sense it as historical human experience. Keep in mind that for Africans witchcraft was an evil within, an antisocial quality, which they often visualized as a corrupt visceral substance. In the African communal ethos of personalized politics, this image represents with particular clarity—or I should say, with characteristic directness—a sense of corruption in the body politic.

People accustomed to the face-to-face intimacy of Africa's domestic economies and societies found the anonymity of strangers anomalous and risky—in a deeply personal way as well as in a material ("business") sense. With merchants from afar, one effected conclusive exchanges by a payoff in cash or trade goods intended to sever any ongoing personal obligation between giver and taker (thereby rendered "buyer" and "seller") rather than consolidate the connection of patron to client, or supplicant to sponsor, fundamental to the ethos of connections. Further, the material gains that individuals made from such transactions violated the fundamental sharing premise of Africa's communal ethos.

Material—as distinct from human—accumulation thus embodied (*sic!*) the fundamental evil of (suspected) betrayal and traffic with aliens, whether "red" Europeans, visiting Muslims, or African strangers. Wealth in things, secretly hoarded for self-aggrandizement, carried overtones of perversion, a bargain with the devil. The relevant distinction was not between "Africans" and Others but between balanced reciprocities among known associates and imbalanced gains from associating with outsiders. Political authorities who built their power on commercialized exchanges with Europeans were accordingly (and their modern counterparts still are) suspected of being witches as well as respected (feared?) as kings. In an alternative metaphor for the same idea of an inner disruption of an outwardly healthy (moral) order, in central Africa local people who achieved eminence by mercantile success joined healing cults to purge themselves of the moral failure implicit in material accumulation achieved by consuming one's relatives and associates.

Most people in Africa accordingly understood the Atlantic commerce as an extreme form of illicit consumption—directly of humans, not commodities: they saw the Europeans as "cannibals." The cowrie shells that constituted the currency of trade in parts of the Gulf of Guinea, they knew, grew on the sunken bodies of captives who drowned or who were thrown into the seaside lagoons on their way out to the import-bearing ships anchored just offshore. And the consummate evil of enslavement itself, being kidnapped and stripped of all the human associations that defined identity, could itself be interpreted as a consequence of witchcraft, of betrayal from within the community of trust. Once the disappearance of intimates stimulated suspicions of this sort within communities, they could heal the wounds and restore social integrity only by condemning others of their own as the witches responsible, thus taking the first step in the process of social ostracism that ended in disposal of outcasts to passing merchants. Some of them ultimately—though often only many transactions later—ended up sold to Europeans at the coast as slaves.

Consider the tragedy of thus seeking the sources of the very local, personal suffering that accompanied (or constituted) Africa's growing engagement with the currents of Atlantic commerce in the confines of the small communities within which most Africans experienced this very broad process: a self-defeating attempt to restore the integrity of a body politic dissolving in dissension and suspicion by purging it of its own human vitality. Describing the process in these African terms immediately suggests (to me, at least) the analogy of contemporary European medicine attempting to cure afflictions recognized as physical by purging bodies with emetics, enemas, and bleedings. And, of course European and American historians are now rewriting the history of their parts of the eighteenth-century Atlantic world in material analogs to the way the Africans characterized the process from the beginning, as a revolution in the "consumption" of things—not of people.

Contemplating the Atlantic era in Africa's history in terms of witchcraft begins to suggest the intensity of the moral crisis that clearly gripped most people there by the late eighteenth century, after more than one hundred years of violent disruptions of community and invisible betrayals of personal trust perpetuated by supposed patrons who in fact sought private advantage at the expense of those dependent on them. One could trust the least those on whom one depended most. Africans would not have thought in terms of such abstractions as "European demand for Africans as slave labor." To my mind, trauma was pervasive and formed the historical context out of which arose not only the internal destructiveness of slaving itself but also many of the often convulsive popular responses of the nineteenth century that presently enter world history textbooks (if at all) only under exoticizing ethnographic or orientalist labels—Muslim *jihads*, "millennial uprisings," and "witchcraft eradication movements."

If the era was a plague of witches for Africans, an eruption of the evil within, and they fought it with witch-hunts and other ultimately self-destructive attempts at social reconciliation, early modern Europe also had its wars of religion, as old Catholic certainties dissolved into the risks and vulnerabilities of Protestant individualism and modern capitalism. Was the well-known flaring of witch-hunts in Europe during the agonized transition from a similarly communal ethic to the individualistic strivings of early capitalism purely coincidental? I would not presume to defend the parallel in detail, but if what we are learning about African history enables one to raise that question about Europe, I think we are poised to develop a validly multicentric world history by bringing Africa in, on Africans' terms, to illuminate what we otherwise haven't seen clearly within our own discourse. "Others," when we see them as who they were rather than as what we need them to have been, become mirrors reflecting truths that we don't otherwise see in ourselves.

On a pan-Atlantic scale, Africans, as the discourse of witchcraft and the recourse to slaving affirmed, had primarily their own human wealth to pay for their investments in developing commercial modernity. Europeans, on the other hand, had the unprecedented specie resources of the Americas, entire continents of productive land in the New World at its disposal, as well as a long lead in individualist accumulation and in literacy-based material technologies, all of which contributed to the decisive capitalist and technological turns taken there. But that's a story that deserves to be told in terms of both historical contingency and the global processes that accommodated these complementing alternative strategies and experiences in Africa (and Asia) of the same long-term historical dynamics. Balanced formulations of conflicts within both the conventionally racialized sides, as well as between them, develop a narrative far more interesting than "blacks" once again in "bondage," a narrative that illuminates both familiar processes in Europe and processes in Africa familiar only to Africanists by setting both in their full, global historical contexts, each including the other (and I've artificially limited my phrasing of the point to take account of only two sides, while in fact there were more, in the Americas and in Asia), each serving as context to explain the other.

As a world historian, I offer this historical vision of early Africa as a contributing center in a balanced array of engaged participants in a multicentered, multilayered, multiply-initiated, and multiply-experienced history —one that goes beyond comparisons of isolated cases of singular abstractions, which mostly reflect the experience of the modern West. This vision also goes beyond the movements of people, crops, animals, germs, and ideas among geographical regions treated as entities otherwise autonomous to include peoples' substantive experiences of processes broader than they could apprehend from within the local or regional (or national) historical contexts in which they lived. Conventional history fails to address fully the fact that people throughout history have reacted to long-term, broad processes of which they were only dimly aware. World historical patterns like these are indeed processes, aspects of the universal human ephemerality of living in time, rather than static institutions; they are significant as history primarily in their dynamic aspects. It is these broad processes, always and only as experienced in specific historical contexts, that world history distinctively considers, in all the multiplicity of their manifestations. From careful consideration of these individual historical experiences—the local in the global (rather than the other way around)—emerge transtemporal and transcultural recurrences not evident from within any of them alone.

It is this particular strength of world history that allows Europeanists to learn more about Europe by understanding places like Africa, Asia, the Americas, or the Pacific on their own terms. How much more fully do we understand England or France in the eighteenth century, for instance, if we take account of the full global context, including Africa? Even Americanists are now discovering that they can't understand the troubled assemblage of the modern United States without appreciating fully the respective backgrounds of the diverse people who confronted one another in North America. It is the responsibility of historians, and the distinctive strength of world historians, to identify the significant aspects of their subjects' lives of which they were unaware. Doing so highlights the contingencies, the shortsightedness, the unintended consequences of what they did, and the ironies and tragedies that make their stories realistic and appealing. World history has no place for the triumphal narrative of the unfolding of inherent superiority—of one race over others, of technological mastery over nature, or of national character—to which regional histories are all but inevitably vulnerable.

Our disciplinary logic particularly depends on contrasting what is unique or momentary with what recurs more generally. So, too, with world history as a distinctive epistemology. History is always about ourselves or about some protagonist with whom the historian and her or his audience identify *against* Others. But for this confrontation to generate historical energy, a genuine dynamic of change, the Others must be given autonomous agency, must be shown to act beyond reaction, acting not only for themselves but also by standards of their own making. I have offered examples of Africans' motivations to suggest how we now can see people of many different sorts interacting there, independently of outsiders, engaged with Muslims as well as Europeans, and with others as well but autonomously so, perhaps "losing" collectively in Europeans' terms, or in the long run, but in the accessible—and hence motivating—short term gaining privately on other terms of their own.

Historically Africans centered their concerns on one another, among the people they knew, on the distinctions of rank and social relationships by which they made themselves and not exclusively (and for most of the past, not even particularly) on their contacts (not "relationships" in their sense) with outsiders, Others whom they displaced to nonhuman spaces. Thus a world history that evaluates Africans only in terms of their relations with others' worlds catches only the most fleeting glimpses of what they were in fact about. World history, despite its patronizingly inclusive impulses to draw selectively on the intermittent evidence of "states," monuments, militarism, and resistance to the eventual European triumph, leaves Africans without motivations—and hence without history—of their own.

That is bad enough for Africans. But the rest of the world is no less impoverished by the absence of their vital counterpoint to the teleology of European triumph. It is of course a truism, or ought to be, that globalization is a dialectical process that stimulates diversity in measures at least equal to the conformity that it threatens. One breathes life back into the gasping body of a world history of triumphal Western modernity—or steadily creeping globalization—only by focusing on the domestic, regional, local histories, and personal biographies of the people who made and continue to make history happen in Africa (or anywhere else.). Then we can build a multiplistic history—or multiple histories—around the ways in which their many and diverse strategies drew on the broader contexts or proceeded innocently of these contexts while nonetheless being part of them.

My final reflections ascend to the level of conviction that Jörn Rüsen has characterized as "moral."[4] We are living with intensifying globalization. Our predecessors have dealt with earlier phases of this fulfillment of the inherently human propensity—I would actually say *need*—to network in intriguingly complex ways. This characteristically incremental process first invented "non-Western" histories by inverting "Western civilization" to study other civilizations in the 1950s and 1960s. Then in the 1970s and 1980s scholars focused on what they saw as non-Western deficiencies ("underdevelopment" and the like), which they tended to blame on the West. The West was inverted from noble and civilizing (later Westernizing and modernizing) to domineering and exploitive. Now, after sensing the autonomous and enormously diverse creativities of human beings all around the globe, extreme constructivists cannot imagine a "there" out there if it is not ours; if our realities are not real, then nothing can really be. But let's be real: the truth is, there are multiple historical realities, the perceptions by which people act and generate change. Historians attempt to sense and to contemplate the relationships among these multiple realities—their own, their readers', their subjects', and the many others among whom their subjects lived. My world history amalgamates these meaningful worlds in a multicentric integration of balanced, engaged, autonomous strivings and misunderstandings. Its tone cherishes failure as much as success and considers thoroughly the standards applied to determine the difference between the two. It is ironic at best and often tragic. It teaches readers to recognize and accept their own all-too-human limitations; it is a badly needed antidote to the hubris of individualism that drives the contemporary world.

Notes

1. Lauren Benton, "How to Write the History of the World," *Historically Speaking* 5 (March 2004): 5.

2. Wyatt MacGaffey, "African History, Anthropology, and the Rationality of Natives," *History in Africa* 5 (1978): 101–20.

3. As phrased artfully by Fred Lee Hord (Mzee Lasana Okpara) and Jonathan Scott Lee, eds., *I Am Because We Are: Readings in Black Philosophy* (Amherst: University of Massachusetts Press, 1995).

4. Jörn Rüsen, "Morality and Cognition in Historical Thought: A Western Perspective," *Historically Speaking* 5 (March 2004): 40–42.

The Way of Africa, "The Way I Am," and the Hermeneutic Circle

Ricardo Duchesne

How refreshing and heartening it is to read an Africanist tell world historians that a valid multicentric world history is a far more complicated endeavor than tracing ecological and commercial connections and comparisons between different global societies. Joseph Miller correctly observes that world historians—notwithstanding their progressive efforts to present Africans "as builders of states and monuments or as members of ethnicized cultures"—have yet to incorporate into their global narratives the "distinctive ways of thinking" of Africans themselves. They have been rather mute, if uninterested, in discussing and learning about the critical, reflexive methodologies that specialists in African history and culture have cultivated over the past few decades. If Miller is aware that world historians no longer ignore but indeed prioritize Africa's long-term interactions with the rest of the world as well as interactions across many cultural borders within Africa, he thinks they are still missing the uniquely creative ways in which Africans have adapted to shifting global circumstances. As critical as world historians have been in their inversion of European history "from noble and civilizing" to "domineering and exploitative," they are still working within the paradigm of modernization and the narratives of individual freedom, the nation-state, and economic development. They are little aware of the methodologies Africanists have cultivated for reconstructing primary accounts of the many different strategies that Africans themselves "invented to work their ways out of specific contradictions" generated by their participation in the Atlantic slave trade.

Miller is not always definitive but his message does come through: the union of Africa and world history requires stepping beyond a liberal, teleological discourse where history is conceived as a progressive process and

From *Historically Speaking* 6 (November/December 2004)

the nonmodern customs, institutions, and modes of thought of the "peoples without history" are judged—in the words of Dipesh Chakrabarty—"in terms of a lack, an absence, or an incompleteness that translates into inadequacy."[1] Miller focuses on the "sensitive issue of African involvement in Atlantic slaving" to highlight the method of understanding needed to bring Africans into a multicentric world history. We need first to appreciate Africa's communal ethos and the idea that one "existed" as an individual to the degree that one affiliated oneself with others and that success in this cultural context meant the accumulation of human connections "through multiple distinctions of age, gender, rank," including the taking of wives, enlisting new clients, enslaving vulnerable strangers, and siring children. Miller further enjoins us to understand Africans not as passive actors who sold what Europeans demanded for their accumulation of capital but as creative agents who adapted their "traditions" to changing circumstances by strategically buying the textiles, alcohol, and guns from the Atlantic as a means of assembling larger connections and, at this historical juncture of new opportunities and escalating competitiveness, by imposing "personal followings on the most dependent terms." Africans were facing a conflict-ridden, intensively competitive reality where the powerful could only survive by escalating the process of controlling people around them. It was out of this reality that powerful Africans eventually created new dynamic "states" in the eighteenth century.

Miller's point is not that African history should be seen on its own terms to the point of isolating it from the modern processes of the "growing Atlantic economy." Africans "participated no less than anyone else" in the development of a global capitalist economy, but they did so in their own way. This way, I might clarify, should not be stereotyped as an incomplete, less-developed historical experience than the more-individualistic but equally violent path the European ruling groups followed in their enclosure movement against customary peasants and in their colonization of the Americas. Miller clearly wants to transcend the legendary Marxist concept of "uneven development" and the fashionable world systems idea of a modern world economy tightly structured by European dynamics.

Another theme that troubles Miller about the narrative of modernization and underdevelopment is the way it sets up a binary opposition between the science and the individualism of Europeans as "objective" and "rational" and the witchcraft and communal practices of Africans as "superstitious" and "irrational." African witchcraft, he intimates, cannot be conceived as the timeless, nonmodern, unreflective behavior of a people unable to understand the new pressures of global circumstances. Within the African communal ethos of personalized thinking and face-to-face intimacy, Miller explains, many Africans were disturbed by the anonymity of the impersonal relations growing in the Atlantic trade exchanges and the material gains that could be achieved by some African individuals from such transactions. By the late eighteenth century, after more than one hundred years of trade with the Atlantic, many individuals had sought to enrich and empower themselves through private commercial exchanges that threatened the competitive strategies of "belonging" and the ethos of collective responsibility. Witchcraft, in this context, was a historical and intentional reaction against supposed patrons who had accumulated wealth in things through impersonal traffic with strangers. If at times witchcraft involved a process of social ostracism that led to the "disposal of outcasts to passing merchants"—some of whom "ended up sold to Europeans at the coast as slaves"—at other times it took the form of successful, private individuals joining "healing cults" as a way of cleansing themselves of the evil forces that had led them to seek success outside the community.

Miller's call upon world historians to bring Africa into the world "on Africans' terms" is an arresting one. He realizes that a world history that accords Africa a central place in the history of European industrialization is still a history that corresponds to a theme of European universalization and does not recognize Africans genuinely in their differences. What troubles me about Miller's essay, however, is its lack of methodological reflexivity. This is all the more ironic in that Miller opens his essay with a citation from Lauren Benton complaining that "world history has not produced a significant volume of methodologically thoughtful discussions."[2] Yet, apart from general remarks about the need to focus "on the domestic, regional, local histories, and personal biographies" of Africans, Miller never addresses the key question of how historians working in Europe and the United States can illuminate "Others" as "who they were rather than as what we need them to have been." I read Miller's long and exciting 1999 presidential address to the American Historical Association, "History and Africa/Africa and History," which is specifically about the historiographies and the methodologies of Africanists, and he does speak here in detail about sources with "distinctively African characteristics," the oral traditions of Africa's past, the use of "powerful linguistic techniques for hearing about the past as Africans experienced it," the ethnographic method, French neo-Marxist anthropology, and the ways these methods were applied by pioneering Africanists in numerous works produced after World War II.[3] But in this address, too, he pays no attention to problems regarding the incommensurability between different cultural traditions with no shared criteria of moral evaluation. He, to the contrary, presumes that the methods employed by Africanists have afforded them with means to enter into the cultural horizon of Africa's past from an autonomous rational perspective that is independent of the traditions of the scholars themselves. What he calls in this address a "humanistic" perspective is really the Enlightenment ideal that one can interpret different traditions from a neutral or universal standpoint without projecting onto Others one's own prejudices.[4] Miller chides Westerners who impose on African history their modern individualistic assumptions, but he does not subject to examination how he (Miller) can reason in Cartesian fashion outside his own cultural context to achieve objective knowledge of the African world on its own terms.

Had Miller been less dismissive of Western culture—"the hubris of individualism"—he might have been willing to consider that only by going through European culture can we learn about the distinctive ways of Africans themselves.[5] He might have noted that alongside the infamous Cartesian outlook, which seeks an unbiased, objective knowledge of the world by separating subject and object, being and thinking, there is a fascinating interpretative or hermeneutic tradition that may be traced back to Giambattista Vico (1668–1744) and Johann Herder (1744–1803) and the world of late eighteenth-century German scholarship. The effort to understand the Other was not initiated by African scholars. This hermeneutic tradition, embraced by the Romantic movement, was articulated as a new method of "higher criticism" by Friedrich Schlegel (1772–1829), who lectured on the philosophy of history and insisted on discovering the original spirit under the letter of a text. It was broadened by the theologian Friedrich Schleiermacher (1768–1834), who argued that the task of interpreters of cultural and linguistic Others was to understand authors better than they understood themselves. But it was Wilhelm Dilthey (1833–1911) who firmly established it in the context of the so-called "explanation-understanding controversy" when he proposed that historical knowledge itself, by contrast to scientific explanations, is obtained hermeneutically through empathetic understanding by working backward through texts to arrive at the original experience of their authors. In the twentieth century the interpretative tradition was expanded and radicalized by Edmund Husserl's phenomenology, Albert Schutz's intersubjective world of meaning, Martin Heidegger's concept of "being-able-to-be-in-the-world," and Ludwig Wittgenstein's language game analysis. It was pushed beyond epistemological concerns about the proper (original) understanding of written documents or speech (which still retained the subject-object duality) toward the idea that all interpretation involves an encounter, a permanent tension between one's own historical horizon and that of the Other. Hans-Georg Gadamer's main work, *Truth and Method* (1960), is particularly credited with the central innovation that understanding is a never-ending process in the form of a conversation between one's own horizon and the horizon of others.

This idea that all interpretation involves a circular process is known as the *hermeneutic circle*. I believe that Miller's interpretation of Africa's way is halfway from completing this circle. If I may use Gadamer's words, Miller understands that to speak of Africa's way "is to see the past in its own terms, not in terms of our contemporary criteria and prejudices but with its own historical horizon." And that "if we fail to transpose ourselves into the historical horizon from which the traditionary text speaks, we will misunderstand the significance of what it has to say to us. . . . We must place ourselves in the other situation in order to understand it." It is "constantly necessary to guard against overhastily assimilating the past to our own expectations of meaning." We must "listen to tradition in a way that permits it to make its own meaning heard." But what Miller ignores is that there are "two different horizons" involved in all interpretations: "the horizon in which the person seeking to understand lives and the historical horizon within which he places himself."[6] Miller is not hermeneutically self-conscious of his own particular cultural background.

Insofar as we want to imagine the other situation, it is necessary, of course, to put ourselves in someone else's shoes, but at the same time it is impossible to escape one's own horizon. The horizon that Miller has assumed unreflectively is that of the neutral, abstract, universal subject of the Enlightenment who disregards his own Western traditions. It is the horizon of the multicultural relativist who is willing to accept all arguments because he believes that all traditions are in principle worthy of the same respect. This is not the way I am.[7] While I agree with Gadamer that it is always possible to adopt more-inclusive positions through cultural conversations, I think it is also consistent with the hermeneutic tradition to feel a commitment to those values that are part of my historical horizon and are constitutive of my identity—values that engender within me a prejudicial disposition toward traditions that fail to meet such standards as freedom of conscience, separation of church and state, respect for the unique identities of each individual, and equality of opportunity. I am attached and accept the truth and the moral superiority of the very tradition that has accustomed me to the idea that I should be willing to hear the arguments of others. Eurocentrism is an intrinsic and acceptable component of evaluation within the hermeneutic circle.

NOTES

1. Dipesh Chakrabarty, *Provincializing Europe: Postcolonial Thought and Historical Difference* (Princeton: Princeton University Press, 2000), 32.

2. Lauren Benton, "How to Write the History of the World," *Historically Speaking* 5 (March 2004): 5. This essay offers no valuable suggestion of its own, at least not for Miller, because it is an endorsement of the very methodologies Miller finds wanting: the "world history connected" approach, which Patrick Manning, Jerry Bentley, Ross Dunn, Philip Curtin, A. G. Frank, William McNeill, and many current world historians have embraced as the most politically correct method of promoting the idea of a common human history long connected through the movements of commodities, capital, ideas, people, and germs (which Benton prefers to call "circulationist"), and the comparative historical approach (which Benton herself uses), long employed by historical sociologists.

3. Joseph C. Miller, "History and Africa / Africa and History," *American Historical Review* 104 (1999): 1–32.

4. Ibid., 24.

5. In truth Miller is comfortably at home with the world-connected approach (read: "world systems" approach) insomuch as it reduces modern European history and culture to the slave trade, the colonization of the non-Western world, and the propagation of germs, alcohol, and guns.

6. For these quoted passages, see Hans-Georg Gadamer, *Truth and Method* (New York: Crossroad, 1989), 300–307.

7. "The Way I Am" is a song on Eminem's second album, *The Marshall Mathers LP.*

Africa in World History and Historiography

Patrick Manning

As Joseph Miller's essay demonstrates, it is still necessary to make the case for the inclusion of Africa in interpretations of world history. Indeed, as he also shows, it is still necessary to make the case for the relevance of world history as a field of study. Most readers are surely predisposed to accept the relevance of world historical analysis and the relevance of Africa and African perspectives within world history. But the devil is in the details, and traces of national, civilizational, and Western-centered perspectives—appropriate, in and of themselves—still tend to devalue the development of a sufficiently lively and coherent field of world history. As ways to address these intellectual constraints, Miller has chosen to focus on African outlooks, on irony and tragedy in history, and on the place of the "face-to-face intimacy" of local initiatives in African and world history.

The overall message is that there should be expanded study of world history, that its approach should be multicentric, and that it should include Africa and the perspectives that one can learn from Africans. I quite agree. Further, Miller intends his argument to respond constructively to Lauren Benton's comment that "world history has not produced a significant volume of methodologically thoughtful discussions or theoretically influential studies." On this point I find that Miller's insights are representative of this early-stage world historical conceptualization, in that they raise more questions than they resolve.

It has been something more than a generation's time since African studies became an organized field of study. Those trained in the early stages of this academic venture are now reaching their full maturity and offering commentaries such as that of Miller. African studies began as an extension

From *Historically Speaking* 6 (November/December 2004)

of humanistic and social science analysis to areas beyond the West. Africa was seen as the region most foreign to the West, and it was the last (along with Southeast Asia) to benefit from organized area-studies programs. One of the tragedies of Africanist scholarship is that scholars born and working in Africa, while they had a promising beginning in the 1960s and 1970s, found their work limited by political conflict, university closures, and structural-adjustment programs. While there has developed a cosmopolitan intellectual consensus among Africanist scholars, it remains the case that scholars of African birth are a clear minority (in contrast, for instance, with East Asianists), and most of the active African-born scholars are expatriates, working especially in North America. These limits on links between Africanist scholarship and contemporary African life cannot be beneficial for the scholarship.

Over time, Africanists on the continent and abroad have developed a remarkable corpus of scholarship, so that African societies and their histories are now known and documented in far greater depth than a generation ago. Many and perhaps most Africanists remain devoted to the study of the continent alone and have no scholarly interest in global affairs. Nevertheless, some Africanist scholars have become steadily more ready to articulate a view of the world, partly because of their intensive analysis of the continent and partly through interaction with scholarship on other regions. In particular, a number of active thinkers in world history come from Africanist backgrounds.

Miller's intervention here focuses on African perspectives in the era of the external slave trade. The advantage of this choice is that it demonstrates a multicentric interpretation of the world that accounts for African perspectives. It shows, through the issue of "witchcraft," that African perspectives may have been not only different in kind but different in social location from state-centered European perspectives. As he implies, this lesson should generalize easily to other regions and provide the basis for a substantial rethinking of early modern world history.

Multicentrism, arguably, is empirically necessary for developing a world history that goes beyond a collection of national histories. Miller's observations, though they clarify the issue of multiple perspectives across the continents, do not yet resolve our problems in interpreting the world and Africa's place within it. Instead, they reveal further complexity. My discussion turns now to identifying some of the difficulties uncovered by Miller's argument.

One difficulty is the place of the historian in articulating past perspectives. In Miller's case (and my own), it is the problem of the historian who has adopted an African identity without abandoning a distant identity given at birth. We seek to identify and articulate the thoughts of past Africans in the discourse of academics today. It is an important but problematic task, involving complex analysis and leaps of faith.

A second difficulty is that of grappling with alterity. The concept is fundamental, beginning with the separation of mother and child. The historian's objective is to identify the reality of difference from "the other" but also to identify wider unities. It is to transform rather than reject the notion of "other." In this case, Miller has sought to replace the stereotypical alterity of blackness, bondage, and blame with a vision of African thought focusing on face-to-face communities.

The tricky effort to summarize a historical situation without essentializing it presents a third difficulty. Miller has developed the concept of "witchcraft" to explain how Africans understood disruptive strangers, to set it in opposition to European thinking. The strength of this approach comes in applying this notion of "witchcraft" to regions around the Atlantic. But I wonder if Miller's summary doesn't come close to asserting a civilization-wide unifying principle. Another approach might have been to focus more on debate within Africa and to contrast debates in Africa with debates in other regions.

There is a need to make general statements about Africa in order to include the continent in a global discourse. But the resulting problems with making general statements about Africa show up in several ways: for instance, in the teaching of world history. World history teachers, focused on connections and comparisons, emphasize leading their students through connections (in commerce, especially) between Africa and other regions. They do indeed connect Africa to Europe, the Americas, and Asia. But then "Africa" comes to be conceived of as a single place—almost as a point. Teachers and students can find little to say about connections between one part of Africa and another in commerce or in other topics.

A fourth difficulty—and this is the one I find most significant—is that multicentrism does not give us immediate progress on the problem of "methodologically thoughtful discussions or theoretically influential studies." In the short run, it compounds the problem by adding dimensions to the analysis without providing an obvious principle for unifying them. In the search for coherent analysis, multicentrism threatens cacophony. I favor pressing ahead, persevering and practicing multicentric history until a logic for it emerges. But I find that we are now in an uncomfortable stage of the process.

I don't claim to have quick answers to these difficulties. My approach has been somewhat parallel to Miller's. In a book on "navigating" world history, I treat African studies as an instructive metaphor for world historical studies.

While I have tended to emphasize a wider range of scales in time, space, and topic than Miller, the basic inspiration provided by African history remains similar. African history provides multiple centers, multiple visions, and unexpected transformations and linkages; it sets a test for those who would treat the past primarily through dominance. But we're still experimenting with how to make sense of larger histories.

The intellectual challenge of our present globalizing era is not that globalization is new—for it is manifestly not new—but that we can no longer afford to ignore it in social scientific analysis. Similarly we can no longer afford to marginalize those who attempt to carry out global historical analysis by dismissing them for the provisional nature of their interpretations. Joseph Miller has forthrightly taken a position within this field of study and is ready to engage in a debate that may carry us toward a stronger global historical analysis. I wish him an interesting and fruitful debate, and I hope we will all benefit from it.

Comment on Miller

William H. McNeill

"**B**eyond Blacks, Bondage, and Blame" skillfully skewers longstanding caricatures of Africa's part in world history and offers some arresting new thoughts about how involvement with the larger world provoked new social and political responses among Africans. But I am not convinced that Joseph Miller is justified in writing about "Africans" in general and across indefinite periods of time exhibiting the same responses. When did Africa enter world history, for example? Not, as he seems to say, in the eighth century. For Africa, as the cradle of humankind, once embraced all the human history there was. And when human groups began to occupy new environments in Asia, Europe, and beyond, Africans retained slender but uninterrupted connections with adjacent peoples as part of a worldwide human web.

Later on, when contacts with Asians and Europeans became more pervasive and disruptive, which is what Miller is thinking of, surely it made a difference whether local Africans were foragers, pastoralists, or farmers. It made a difference, too, how firmly local communities were connected with those around them, that is, what local webs of exchange and patterns of social differentiation had arisen and what sorts of local and individual skills had emerged.

By the time Asian and European influences became apparent and disruptive to older styles of life, most Africans were farmers, living in villages, and that was where a mounting stream of novelties impinged on their lives, some coming from afar, some generated nearby or within the village itself. That implies an infinite, or effectively infinite, local variety of experiences, seldom or never recorded. How, then, can historians hope to know what really happened among Africans in general and common folk in particular?

This is no trivial question and applies with equal force to European, Asian, and Amerindian history. The great majority of humankind in the deeper past left no written records behind and still does not. And travelers' reports and the like are liable to gross misunderstanding, thanks to linguistic and conceptual barriers between observer and observed. Even, if Miller is to be believed, the supposedly sensitized and sympathetic anthropologists of the last hundred years or so interpreted what they saw and heard to suit themselves and according to ideas they brought with them.

Yet human minds, using words, find (invent? impose?) patterns amid the confusing variety of actual sensory experience and act as though these are real. This indeed is the secret of our extraordinary biological and technological success: getting results we like by acting in concert in the light of agreed-upon meanings. Cooperation was sometimes conscious and voluntary, but often it was the opposite—a more or less desperate effort to protect old ways against betrayers within and against strangers from outside the local community. The process Miller discusses whereby Muslim and European influences infiltrated Africa after the eighth century was part of that process, affecting the lives of all parties to the encounter in ways seldom recorded and only dimly understood at the time or subsequently. So how can we know? In all probability, the best effort of historians and other observers today to comprehend what happened will seem as inadequate to future generations as Miller tells us the views of older generations of African historians are to him—and to me.

Yet no one is satisfied by confessing ignorance. Better a caricature of reality to believe in than a blank; and that is what Miller's bold strokes and sweeping generalizations offer us. Mind you, he really deals only with West Africa and the centuries when the transatlantic slave trade was in spate. He thus perpetuates some of the narrowness he ridicules in his first pages: for he, too, focuses on African responses to Europeans, as well as on slavery, with all the distaste for that form of human exploitation that we take for granted.

Being of much the same professional background as Miller, I find his general ideas attractive, in particular his account of African sociopolitical patterns and his interpretation of witchcraft. His dismissal of *tribe* as a meaningful term and counter-suggestion that Africans sought power "by controlling the efforts of the people around them, through multiple distinctions of age, gender, rank, among other means of differentiations—increasingly after 1700 or so, including slavery" seems convincing to me even when recognizing how impossible it is for him or anyone else really to know how millions of actual persons felt and thought and acted.

Parallel challenges to older forms of society and community solidarity had arisen among other peoples exposed to contact with powerful, specially skilled outsiders from the time when cities and civilizations first differentiated themselves from their agrarian hinterlands. Miller's hint that similar processes dominated northern and western Europe in the early Middle Ages deserves development, for it is true that between the third and ninth centuries, older "barbarian" patterns of life broke down throughout Germanic Europe as new "tribes" and warlords engaged in slaving and conquest, and new states slowly and painfully emerged, along with a new religion and an accompanying legal-moral code. Breakdown and painful reintegration into a wider world continued to occur along the fringes of Europe into the eighteenth century. In 1745 my own ancestors, for example, were caught up in this process when they fought under the clan chief at Culloden in vain defense of a crumbling old regime.

Miller's second major thesis, that "'witchcraft' (N.B.: *our* designation of the experience) provided the terms in which most people in Africa experienced the human exploitation of this era," seems plausible, too, though I wonder about competing worldviews—Islam in particular, which surely played some part in West Africa long before European traders appeared along that coast. Apprenticeship to imported faiths was indeed confined to ruling and mercantile circles to begin with. The same was true in Germanic Europe when Christianity first began to spread there. But the legal and moral codes carried by Islam and Christianity from the urban contexts within which they arose were of key importance for the long-term reorganization of society in Europe and, I believe, also in West Africa. Both societies had to learn to accommodate the initial shock of the immorality of trade and of the "material gains that individuals made from such transactions [that] violated the fundamental sharing premise of Africa's communal ethos."

In general, it seems to me that Miller slights the Muslim presence in Africa. Plunging toward the folk level, where the majority most certainly existed, he relies on inference and imagination to construct his version of "witchcraft," neglecting the imported missionary faiths that were already present and played a more constructive role over the long run than "a self-defeating attempt to restore the integrity of a body politic . . . by purging it of its own human vitality."

Again, many other desperate peoples invented local cults and practices that proved to be vain and self-defeating. Cargo cults in the South Pacific and ghost dances among American Indians are best known. Miller's West African "witchcraft" is another case, previously unknown to me, but all the more plausible because it conforms so closely to human responses among others in parallel situations.

My reaction to Miller's essay therefore boils down to two suggestions. First, his portrait of West Africa's painful encounter with the rest of the world after 1600 or so would become more interesting and persuasive if he were to compare what happened there explicitly with similar older and contemporary patterns elsewhere. Second, I also feel that by dismissing "a revolution in the 'consumption' of things" as just another ploy on the part of Western historians to denigrate Africans he is making a mistake. The arrival of American food crops and the role of African diseases in safeguarding African societies against more rapid disintegration were of major importance for those concerned. Maize and peanuts are not universal in Africa, but they are significant food crops today and probably became so in the eighteenth century. Guns, too, changed war and politics in far-reaching ways by giving a new advantage to those who got possession of them. And, as I said before, religious ideas with concomitant notions of law, property, and justice imported from afar played no small part in changing African society, dating back to initial encounters with Christianity in northeast Africa in the second century and with Islam in the seventh century.

All human contact and communication inaugurate a two-way process by provoking borrowing on both sides, with subsequent adaptations, misunderstandings, actions, and reactions. By emphasizing African distinctiveness—local forms of social solidarity and power through accumulating a following, and the role of "witchcraft"—Miller describes part, but only part, of the encounter. New crops altered lives also by expanding food supplies, and new ideas borrowed and modified from those outsiders surely changed lives as well.

I could not agree more with Miller's parting observation: "Conventional history fails to address fully the fact that people throughout history have reacted to long-term broad processes of which they were only dimly aware." That means that written sources seldom offer explicit evidence of what world historians most want. Consequently they must rely on an acute and informed imagination to discern the "long-term broad processes" they seek. Miller's essay is a magnificent example of such historical imagination in action. My complaint rests on its partiality. He needs to fly higher, look at Africa as a whole (from Cape of Good Hope to the Mediterranean coastline), consider relations among diverse peoples within that continent and their varied encounters with Islam and peoples of the Indian Ocean coastlines as well as with Europe, and, finally, also go back in time, that is, become a real world historian for whom the painful episode of transatlantic slavery is not the sole—or at least not the overriding—center of his attention. Only by doing so will he really live up to his title by going "Beyond Blacks, Bondage, and Blame."

Finding Africa in World History

David Northrup

Joseph Miller's essay contains much to agree with, many points to ponder, and some bits to scratch one's head about. One can enthusiastically
endorse the central thesis that historians need to move beyond externally generated and Eurocentric perspectives that treat sub-Saharan Africans in terms
of their skin color, their prominence in modern slavery, and the legacy of guilt
that slavery and discrimination have left in the Western world. Getting Africa
right can also help refine the larger framework of world history.

While addressing his topic as an Africanist and as a world historian,
Miller appears more comfortable in the former role. He criticizes world history for its lack of theoretical depth and originality, for outmoded "civilizational" and triumphalist Eurocentric approaches, and for not appreciating
Africa on its own terms. World history is also praised for its potential to rise
above such failings, but his essay is more inclined to emphasize what world
historians should learn from historians of Africa than what Africanists might
learn from world history. In my view, the situation is not one-sided. Some
historians of Africa have also not broken free from conceptual limitations,
and the best of recent world history scholarship is rather more advanced than
the criticisms Miller repeats from Lauren Benton suggest.

Two other aspects of Miller's general argument are both thought provoking and puzzling. One is how to bring Africa into world history, not just on
Africa's terms but also on world history's terms. The "domestic, regional, and
local histories" of African societies and individuals are important components
of good African history, but is world history just the sum of the separate histories of each continent, society, and individual told from their own perspectives? A larger conceptual framework seems necessary to sort out themes and
issues, even if no meganarrative can hope to free itself from all conceptual

From *Historically Speaking* 4 (September 2002)

limitations and cultural prejudices, nor should it need to. Most of those drawn to world history (and continental history) are fleeing fields that prize research of high technical accuracy about isolated topics of limited significance. World historians turn those priorities on their head, valuing broad significance and scope above all and accepting that such goals make complete accuracy very difficult, especially at first crack. They believe posing a good question is more important than being able to answer it satisfactorily. This is not to say that world historians need be content with mediocrity or tied to the kind of conceptual frameworks that Miller justly criticizes. Each of these approaches enabled world historians to move a certain distance down the path of understanding; most world historians have been able to move on from them precisely because they have learned to frame questions better.

Moreover, good historians and good anthropologists have long been aware that the way to improve one's theoretical understanding is through good fieldwork (which Miller endorses) and meaningful efforts to compare approaches across cultures (which Lauren Benton's recent essay stresses is essential to good world history). To advance global understanding, one needs to see people both from their own perspectives and from comparative ones, whose unfamiliarity or unflattering light may sometimes make them wince. The problem seems neatly posed in Miller's suggestion to use "witchcraft" (Europeans' not Africans' term) as a way to understand Africans' responses to the disruptions of slave trading. He rightly draws attention to cultural cosmologies and suggests that fears of malevolent forces were not unique to Africa. On the other hand, what are the comparative implications of placing so much emphasis on the role of the irrational (or differently rational) in understanding Africa? Was Africa fundamentally different in its responses, or should divine providence and witchcraft receive greater emphasis as explanatory frameworks throughout the world?

A second juicy issue that Miller's essay raises is the size and fixity of cultural units in world history. His use of "black" suggests that his "Africa" is sub-Saharan and that he considers North Africans separate in more ways than just geographically. His repeated references to the perspectives of "most people in Africa" permits him to avoid the problem of presenting Africans as an undifferentiated mass, while affirming the existence of a common African experience and cultural framework. In taking such an approach, Miller would not be the first Africanist to press with equal vigor the case for Africa's diversity and the case for its unity. In separate volumes written in the 1960s, for example, anthropologist Jacques Maquet argued that black Africans possessed broad cultural unity that he called "Africanity" and that sub-Saharan Africans could be understood as belonging to six different "civilizations."[1] Maquet acknowledged the tension between these two approaches but argued that they reflected different frames of reference.

Despite such precedents, Miller's vision of sub-Saharan Africans as united by a common history is somewhat unusual among recent historians of Africa, who have been moving away from writing continental or even regional history, as is evident from the titles of most recent monographs and articles in the *Journal of African History*. Even African history textbooks generally write of African "civilizations" in the plural and recount the continent's past largely in regional terms, at least until the colonial conquest. If the textbooks' regions are pretty much the cardinal compass points, their "civilizations" vary considerably in number and defining criteria. Decades ago, Melville J. Herskovits proposed a division of the continent, largely on ecological grounds, into ten culture areas, which Maquet modified into six civilizations below the Sahara. More recently John Thornton has proposed that early modern Atlantic Africa consisted of six (or seven) cultural divisions, but that is quite exceptional. Most recent historians of Africa have found little validity or utility in large cultural units.

Thus, while it is fair to criticize most world historians for focusing too much on state building, migration, and imperialism in their treatment of Africa, it seems equally justified to point out that most historians of Africa have been more concerned with uncovering the details of the small part of the continent that interests them than with clarifying larger regional or continental themes. Miller is to be praised for bucking this trend, even if his "witchcraft" theme looks suspiciously like his work on west-central Africa projected a bit too large.

On the other hand, perhaps world historians would do better to divide up Africa (and other continents) into regions when looking for trends and examining links with other places. Much good work has already been done using maritime units as the focus of analysis. North and northeast Africa share historic ties both to the Mediterranean and to the Middle East. Miller and others have shown the utility of exploring Africa's transatlantic connections, while an Indian Ocean framework has also been effective in incorporating eastern Africa into world history. Despite some limitations, such approaches emphasize important transcontinental exchanges and avoid the pitfalls of demonstrating the existence of pan-African commonalities.

Rather than elaborating on the value of dismembering continental constructs in favor of interacting regions, the remainder of this brief response will sketch some ways in which still broader comparative approaches can illuminate both African and world history. The problem of cultural unity and diversity is not unique to Africa. The apparent unity of Chinese, Indic, or European "civilizations" commonly presented in textbooks and global surveys dissolves upon closer examination into many different cultures. Thus the first insight Africa might provide to the teaching of world history (and vice versa) is a healthy regard for the fact that meganarratives are constructions that, however useful, are selective and oversimplified.

On the other hand, precisely defined concepts can enhance comparative insights. Whereas "civilizations" were once taken to represent advances of some places in the world over "barbarism," most historians now use the term as a synonym for culture, making it easy to find one or many civilizations in Africa and all the other continents. Democratizing "civilization" frees historical surveys from invidious civilized/uncivilized dichotomies but blurs significant cultural differences. An older view of "civilization," devised to describe ancient empires, stressed the cultural unity, not of entire societies or regions but of elite minorities that were trained in a particular assemblage of ideas, skills, aesthetics, language, and literacy. The power of these great traditions (once called "high cultures") among the privileged few gave ancient China, Mesopotamia, India, or Rome their apparent cultural unity and left important legacies to the ages that followed. In their concern to fight older pre-judices that demeaned Africans as "uncivilized" (in a different sense of the term), modern historians of Africa have avoided addressing the significance in sub-Saharan Africa of the lack of literacy and other aspects of a great tradition.

A simplified model of this is a sandwich. The bottom slice is the common cultural substratum, the Africanity that underlay the continent. In an insightful but neglected essay, anthropologist Igor Kopytoff has suggested a historical origin for such cultural unity in the dispersal of peoples to the Nile Valley, North Africa, and below the Sahara, which was set in motion by the desiccation of the Sahara in early antiquity. The Bantu diffusion farther spread closely related languages and cultural complexes over a wide area.[2] Kopytoff's ancient cultural dispersal initially fostered cultural commonalities over a wide area, but the passage of time created myriad variations among dispersed communities. Later, borrowings and interactions among societies added new cultural changes. These cultural variations are the sandwich's filling. Until recent centuries most of sub-Saharan Africa was an open-faced sandwich. This is not a defect, but it is a difference from other ancient societies that developed a great tradition, a top slice on the sandwich, helping to hold its diversity in place through indoctrination of the powerful few in canonical texts and aesthetic forms.

Of course, a sandwich model is much too simple and static. Great traditions have a way of migrating downward in societies, becoming part of the substratum, as Greco-Roman traditions did in the West. One might say that in recent decades Western societies have taken on a more open-faced, or multicultural, look. Meanwhile, sub-Saharan Africans were acquiring great traditions. In his video series, *The Africans,* and the companion volume of the same name, Ali A. Mazrui makes the important point that Africans today have a "triple heritage"—African, Islamic, and European. Rather than emphasizing the alien nature of "outside" contacts, his approach stresses the complex, interactive roles that Africans played in engaging global forces and making them their own. In contrast to Samuel Huntington's model of isolated, clashing civilizations, Mazrui points out that most Africans comfortably blend a substratum of Africanity with a superstratum of Islamic or Western culture or even make a triple-decker sandwich of all three. Those with a comparative bent will easily see that Mazrui's model has great applicability to understanding both cultural change in societies elsewhere in the world and the complex dynamics of contemporary globalization.

The delight of history is its flexibility. One can emphasize continuity or change, unity or diversity, always keeping in mind that these are not opposites but different aspects of a complex web. Bringing Africa into world history raises many intriguing questions, such as how useful the great tradition model may be or whether most of the premodern world was not more like Africa than imperial Rome. Bringing in Africa also makes it easier to invite in others who were once dismissed as "barbarians," "nomads," and "primitive" peoples and relegated to positions outside the gates of history. In so doing, historians should recognize significant differences without wallowing in exaggerated egalitarianism. Bringing world history into Africa may raise difficult questions, but, as Miller shows, it can also lead to useful dialogues.

NOTES

1. Jacques Maquet, *Africanity: The Cultural Unity of Black Africa* (New York: Oxford University Press, 1972) and *Civilizations of Black Africa* (New York: Oxford University Press, 1972). French editions of both had appeared earlier, in 1967 and 1962, respectively.

2. Igor Kopytoff, "The Internal African Frontier: The Making of African Political Culture," in *The African Frontier: The Reproduction of Traditional Societies,* ed. Igor Kopytoff (Bloomington: Indiana University Press, 1987), 3–84.

The Borders of African and World History

Jonathan T. Reynolds

In his thoughtful essay, Joseph Miller provides a stinging critique of how the dominant paradigms of world history have marginalized and even misrepresented the history of Africa. In particular, he identifies world history's emphasis on civilizational units of analysis and its preoccupation with states as having done a disservice to Africa. Well-meaning historians, from the earliest pioneers of the field to recent scholars, argues Miller, have sought to "play by European rules" and legitimize African history by finding African equivalents to European states and empires. Miller states that this approach "trades on (by playing off) precisely the modern, often implicitly racial, distortions that exclude Africa from a history of the world that might include Africans' own visions of struggle and accomplishment."

This is strong stuff. Miller is trying to go beyond the surface "what" of world history and counterpose an African "why" against what he sees as dominant European "why." In so doing, Miller wants historians to take note that there are many "whys" that must be considered when doing world history—hence the idea of being "multicentric." To support his point, he draws upon two key topics: African political systems and African understandings of the Atlantic slave trade. In the case of African political systems, Miller posits that while these structures may appear similar to the states of Europe, they are really very different critters, defined, in Miller's own words, by "a dynamic process of personal interaction rather than relationships stabilized by 'hegemony' or 'legitimacy' or any of the other modern fictions necessary to explain 'structures' that work by abstraction rather than through continuous, real-time confrontation and collaboration." Further, he stresses that the

From *Historically Speaking* 6 (November/December 2004)

misguided quest to find historical "states" in Africa has led to a historical over-emphasis on and misrepresentation of such historical cases as ancient Egypt, Nubia, Ghana, Mali, Songhai, and ancient Zimbabwe.

Miller further argues that to understand the African experience of the slave trade, we must embrace the reality of witchcraft as the lens through which Africans witnessed the "corruption in the body politic" that resulted from "material—as distinct from human—accumulation thus embodied [*sic*] the fundamental evil of (suspected) betrayal and traffic with aliens, whether 'red' Europeans, visiting Muslims, or African strangers." Thus, by examining the slave trade via African eyes, historians can get beyond "bondage" (and per-haps also "blame"?) or "such abstractions as 'European demands for Africans as slave labor'" and appreciate that for Africans the trade was understood as a "moral crisis" in distinctly African terms.

One of the key issues that all who dare to do world history must struggle with is the question of human similarity and difference. "Lumpers" argue that all people are basically similar and can be understood using similar con-cepts and questions. "Splitters" see peoples in different times and places as basically incomparable. In arguing his point for understanding Africa, Miller has placed himself firmly in the splitter camp. Indeed, despite the fact that he expresses his discontent with the "civilizational" approach to world history, he nonetheless argues for the distinctiveness of things African. As he states in his second paragraph: "Africans . . . have had, and have, distinctive ways of think-ing of themselves and their world(s), as well as about the greater world they share with us." On page 9 he returns to this theme and identifies "Africa's communal ethos" wherein ". . . individuals 'existed' not because they could think, alone, for themselves . . . but rather because they affiliated themselves with consummate flexibility with others around them." From this starting point Miller develops his perspectives on African political forms ("states") and the African understanding of the slave trade.

While I agree with much of what Miller has to say, I am nonetheless uncomfortable with the underlying characterization of Africans as "differ-ent." Indeed, in trying to escape the European paradigm of world history, Miller has created a rather selective model of Africa that does not, to me, seem terribly representative of African diversity. Certainly there are plenty of cases where such issues as "legitimacy" were crucial both to African rulers and ruled. Are we really wrong to call the likes of ancient Aksum or Benin states? Perhaps Miller is uncomfortable with the likes of these (or for that matter ancient Egypt or Songhai) because they don't fit his own model of African politics. Similarly, while many Africans may have understood the chaos engendered by the slave trade as witchcraft, many others saw the trade as an exchange of human capital for material capital. Certainly the populations of busy slave ports didn't fear Europeans as outsiders. The appropriation of European identities by many African commercial families suggests just the sort of flexibility of identity that Miller stresses. But if identity is so flexible, then might not the ways in which the great variety of people known collectively as Africans constructed and understood their worlds be flexible, too? I am uneasy with any argument that reduces Africans (or any other continental or racial group) to "people who think like _____." Perhaps Africa is itself large enough to be multicentric.

The notion of an African identity or perspective takes us, I believe, to a critical issue. Can we even use continents such as Africa as units of analysis in world history? Certainly the title of this forum would suggest that we can. However, I suspect that doing so can be misleading, unless it is done with great care. In the remaining space available to me, I would like to examine this issue using the concept of "borders" to guide us through the ways we construct Africa and relate African history to world history.

Borders make us think of geographical constructions, and it is no surprise that our most basic understanding of Africa is as a shape on a map. Further, it seems obvious that people on the same landmass should have much in common—being separated as they are from other people by seas and oceans. This logic lies at the core of the area studies system of learning about the world. But sometimes things that seem obvious are also misleading. Is everything that has happened in Africa really "African" in a way that is historically meaningful, especially at the macro world-history level? Would a thirteenth-century Moroccan salt merchant really share a core "Africanity" with a Khoi-khoi pastoralist of the same era? If not, is one then more "African" than the other? It is a serious question. Might each not have more in common with other people elsewhere in the world? Moreover, since land often separates more effectively than water, perhaps coastal peoples share more with coastal peoples on other continents than with the peoples who dwell in the interior of their own. Maybe the Swahili of the thirteenth century shared certain things in common with other Indian Ocean types that they did not with fellow Africans elsewhere on the continent. The same sort of thing must, of course, be said for other parts of the world. Europe is every bit as modern a notion as is Africa. These constructions might mean something to us now, but can they be applied to the past without misleading our audiences?

Using continents as a unit of analysis leads to textbooks that follow a rather vapid "meanwhile, in Africa" organization—a strategy that literally

divides people who may have much in common. Similarly a continental construction of Africa deals poorly with the movement of populations in and out
of the continent. Does everyone who settles on African soil become African?
When Africans go to Brazil, do they become "South American"? We know it
isn't that simple. Let's face it, continents are the blunt instruments of historical analysis. They can get the job done, but the results are going to be pretty
messy.

If continental boundaries aren't a terribly precise way of defining Africa,
what are our other options? For many, race has served as an alternative. In the
words of reggae artist Peter Tosh: "Don't care where you come from; as long
as you're a black man you're an African." A racial model of Africa has greater
flexibility than a continental one. Anywhere you have black people, you have
African history, simply in diaspora. Such an approach, however, essentializes
Africa and Africans and has the undesirable result of defining anybody
who isn't black as "not African" and thus as an outsider. Books such as Chan-
cellor Williams's *Destruction of Black Civilization: Great Issues of a Race from
4500 B.C. to 2000 A.D.* clearly present an image of a black Africa invaded by
outsiders—first Arabs and then Europeans. But can any such racialized history be seen as a legitimate part of world history? Certainly we have rejected
old-fashioned racist (read "white") versions of world history, such as that of
James Henry Breasted's *Conquest of Civilization.* Can we then embrace a definition of Africa that relies on blackness? Still, many scholars utilize categories such as "black Africa" as a euphemism for "real Africa" (Hegel's "Africa
proper") and place North Africa under the purview of "the Middle East." Yet
the fact that so many job advertisements in African and Middle Eastern history overlap is evidence of the fuzzy border between these units of analysis.

Is there a more effective way to define Africa and Africanness than via
geography or race? Many, including Miller, have argued for a cultural definition of Africanness. As we have already seen, Miller embraces the notion of
a "communal ethos" that defines African political expressions and, more specifically, African understandings of the slave trade. Many Afrocentrists also
embrace a more cultural than racial definition of Africanity, stressing such
elements as matriliny, divine kingship, and ancestor worship as hallmarks of
African culture. Notably the identification of common cultural traits in
ancient African history is a key aspect of the Afrocentric argument for the
existence of an ancient African culture and, hence, an African identity. Even
more than the racial definition of Africa, the cultural model provides a high
degree of flexibility, allowing historians to trace the flow of cultural elements
into and out of Africa. These elements can travel independently of Africans,

via such mechanisms as food, religion, art, literature, and music. And who can doubt the incredible influence of such African cultural elements on the world over the past few hundred years? Yet, reflecting the function, if not the form, of the racial model of Africa, adherents of this cultural definition often see any introduction of "non-African" traits as a process of "de-Africaniza-tion," Thus, if Africans convert to Islam and embrace patrilineal succession, then they have become to some degree "less African." Such a perspective sug-gests that culture is a zero-sum game. If one cultural element is adopted, then another must be lost. In my view, this is a very misleading notion of culture.

The final question, of course, is where do all these constructions of Africa leave us as Africanists and world historians? My argument, if taken to its logi-cal extreme, is that Africa is no less a construction than race. This, though, does not mean that Africa isn't meaningful. Race may be a social construc-tion, but it is one that has played a profound role in world history, and the same can be said for Africa. Even more important, there are several compet-ing constructions of Africa that are available to world historians. The "bor-ders" of Africa I have examined here can have meaning for world history. The key is to present Africa in all its complexity. Scholars need to examine how these constructions overlap and interact. Africa has many roles to play in world history, not the least of which is to get us to think very critically about why we divide up and understand the world the way we do. Thanks are owed to Joseph Miller for helping us to do so.

What Are World Histories?

Michael Salman

J oseph Miller expresses misgivings about the methodological and theoretical foundations of world history in two registers. "As an Africanist," he voices concern that the treatment of Africans by "self-styled" world historians offers "the extreme examples of the exclusion that conventional untheorized standards of world history impose . . . on most of the world." And, "as a historian," he worries that "most world historians . . . seem also to mute, if not negate, central principles of history's distinctive methodology" by emphasizing the origins and continuity of civilizations, rather than attending to change over time in highly contingent and particular contexts. Thus Miller's critique of world history is global in a double sense. It is based on a firm view of what the discipline of history is all about, its "central principles," its purpose, its goals. And his critique is also global in its commitment to inclusion. Indeed, quite admirably, he wants not just inclusion but a historiography turned upside down—a historiography in which, to borrow a culturally laden phrase, the last (to be included in world history) shall be first in leading the way to new understandings of old topics.

Allow me to speak confessionally. I have not styled myself a world historian. Like Miller, I am skeptical about the concept of world history, its claims to go beyond earlier forms of ("Western") civilizational or regional history, and its growing status as a field. I think we might usefully ask not just what kind of world history we want to see, but, more fundamentally, what is world history? Is it a field of history? And what does it mean to be a field of history? As you might begin to guess, I am skeptical about most things. This habit of mind can be tiring. Sometimes it is necessary to accept a given framework and teach one's classes as a matter of practical necessity. We must always make choices and, in that light, the choice of an inclusive world history strikes me

From *Historically Speaking* 6 (November/December 2004)

as a better option than many others that preceded it. However, with regard to world history, there are some specific reasons why I remain a skeptic.

World history, as most commonly practiced, tends to emphasize certain historical narratives almost exclusively. The world is a big place, and it is an old one, too, with lots of internal divisions and cantankerous inhabitants. One might think there would be copious stories to tell. Quite the contrary. The more historians stand back to tell the grandest of grand narratives, the more they focus on selections from just a few story lines. These overweening narratives include stories about the rise and fall of civilizations recognized as "great" and stories about globalizing processes, such as the spread of capitalism, the integration of world markets, natural history (disease, climate, environment), and globalized relations of production. Let me say immediately that these are important histories. I should hope this would be so obvious that no one could misunderstand my critical words as suggesting that these histories should be dismissed. They are necessary histories, but they are often inadequate, never complete, and they should not always occupy the central place in our historical intellect and imagination.

I share Miller's concern about the way that world history tends to represent a modernist and "Western" view of the world, which has trouble with the difficult task of providing satisfying histories of peoples, societies, and cultures that did not (or do not) operate within that model. The problem is not so much that world history tends to convey only a few tremendously important historical narratives among a world full of stories but that it represents just a slender slice of the many different ways of understanding the world historically and understanding how the world has been understood across history and across different cultures in history.

Despite my skeptical arm's-length distance from world history, I share with Miller an interest in what world history is trying to do. This is so for a variety of reasons: because I do style myself as a historian interested in comparative history and epistemology, transnational histories, and translocal processes; because studying "Western" or any other sort of civilization by itself strikes me as a practical, political, and philosophical mistake; and also because I suspect that world history is a little bit like war, in the sense that although you might not be interested in it, as Trotsky once quipped, it is very likely to become interested in you. Not only do the world historical processes of globalization, led by capitalism, seek out new nooks to open and old crannies to expand but some world historians present themselves as historians of the world, swallowing it up in an act of authority so that they (not infrequently Europeanists) can continue to speak authoritatively about the mission of history. They might exclude Africa—or Southeast Asia, a region on which I focus—or they might package its meaning in less than satisfying ways. In the case of exclusion, there seems to be just silence and darkness, while in the case of inclusion there are more clearly questions to be asked about who speaks for whom, with what (or whose) concepts and terminologies.

Too often world history is just "Western" civilization (or a version of European history) partnered with the shadows of other places' and peoples' pasts. Other times it is only a history of the leading processes of modern history swamping over the rest of the world, such as capitalism, the emergence and spread of nationalism, and the dominance of the bureaucratic state. I concur with Miller's call for a fuller inclusion of Africa in world history, just as I would for Southeast Asia. This must be an inclusion that highlights Africans as thinking, speaking, acting subjects who participate in history according to their particular conceptions of their changing contexts, rather than as passive objects swept into larger processes or as actors whose logics and concepts are assumed to be universal and thus identical to everyone else's. But let us ask the more fundamental questions: What constitutes world history? What makes a history a world history?

One traditional answer is that world history is the history of processes and events that have a global impact or significance. This is what Hegel meant when he used the term *world historical,* although Hegel did not mean this in a literally global way because he thought the world was divided between peoples without history (Africans), those whom time had passed by (almost everyone else), and a lucky few (mainly in northwestern Europe) who were the vanguard of the unfolding of universal history. In Miller's examples, we see a different sort of world history revolving around Africans' incorporation into the expanding commercial world of early modern capitalism, primarily through the Atlantic Ocean trading system. What Miller introduces for historians not trained as Africanists is a set of narratives about how and why Africans became involved in this globalizing economy according to their own distinctive ideas about such relationships as rank, status, exchange, identity, authority, and power. It is a world history that does not assume that modern European notions explain everything, and yet it is a world history because it charts a process that is perceived to draw peoples into a globalized history—the history of the expansion of capitalism, its relationships, and its effects.

The main point I would like to make is that this is not the only way to think about world history. As Charles Beard once said, the word *history* always has two meanings: what happened in the past and the study of the past. Twisting Beard just a bit, and perhaps my friend Joe Miller's beard, too,

I think Miller's critique of world history emphasizes the former meaning. Miller deploys methodological and critical acumen to come up with a better world history. As he says, "Given the racial politics of history in Africa, there is an urgency about doing it right, not only doing right by people in Africa (and by their descendants in the diaspora who claim its heritage as their own) but also moving historical epistemology beyond its preoccupation with triumphal progress and toward the more ironic, even tragic, story of all humanity." The injunction to do "it right" reflects a concern for accuracy and justice, but, like the notion that world history should be "the . . . story of all humanity," it also suggests a certain singularity when thinking about history. This singularity does not fit well with a conception of history as itself a culturally and historically situated way of thinking about the past or with similarly contingent conceptions of the world and its diversity of peoples and stories.

Consider the diversity of stories people tell about "all humanity." For example, creation stories are culturally specific. For Jews and Christians who attend to the Old Testament, the first woman, Eve, was created from Adam's rib. For Muslims who attend to the Koran, that story is part of the lore of the older prophets that was discarded to make room for what strikes me as a better story about man and woman being created from the same soul. In the Philippines there are a number of creation stories, including one about Malakas and Maganda, the strong (man) and the beautiful (woman) who emerged from a split stalk of bamboo. Let's stick with this tiny sampling of creation stories. It is enough for us to see just how interesting it can be to contemplate the story of all humanity as a congeries of stories in history.

By the eighteenth century most people in the Philippines had become Christians, at least nominally, and the story of Adam and Eve was fast on its way to being widely known, right alongside the story of Malakas and Maganda, which also persisted. By the next century, about 90 percent of the population was Christian, and presently the figure is roughly 95 percent. Throughout this time, and since before Magellan's ill-fated landing in 1521, about 5 percent of the population has been Muslim and thus possessed of their own multiple stories about all of humanity. Meanwhile, over the last couple of centuries in the Philippines and elsewhere, some Jews, Christians, and Muslims have, like me, become persuaded of vaguely Darwinian ideas about evolution, diminishing the stock we put in other creation stories but not displacing them out of our thoughts. Ferdinand and Imelda Marcos had themselves infamously depicted as Malakas and Maganda in a painting they hung in Malacanang Palace. Probably all Filipinos know a story about all of humanity that matches at least one of these permutations, and there are many who could tell multiple stories encompassing all of these permutations.

Nevertheless, the story of Malakas and Maganda remains culturally specific, or at least relatively so since there are outsiders like me who have learned to tell the story to create critical meaning and intelligence about the past.

Creation stories are just one variant of history, but they usefully illustrate the way that history is a rambunctious dialogue with the past. To be multi-centric rather than dualistic, we might even consider history to be a cacophony about the past. This does not mean that there is no such thing as accuracy or that anyone should jettison the idea of getting history right. I propose an alternative way of thinking about world history as an additive to the discussion, not a displacement. World history is not just the story of the world's past. It should also be about the histories that are told in a world of people who have stories about the past. Just as Miller shows us how a culturally mindful integration of African history into world history can enrich historical thought more broadly, I believe the same is true of a more pluralistic acceptance of different ways of telling stories about the past.

We might understand professional canons of historical practice more fully if we reflect on their differential constitution and application in a plurality of contexts. Among Southeast Asianists in the United States and Europe, for example, there was an imperative in the 1960s and after to seek to explain the truly Southeast Asian concepts around which societies were organized, rather than focus on superficial foreign encrustations like the idea of a nation. Historians in Southeast Asian countries like the Philippines continued to write national histories because these were meaningful to their readers, but American and European authorities tended to look down on them as forever a step behind. National histories were passé in the American academy, they were called "bad history" by some leading historians of Southeast Asia—until a Southeast Asianist named Benedict Anderson drew on the history, politics, and literature of Southeast Asia to inspire *Imagined Communities: Reflections on the Origins and Spread of Nationalism* (1983), a book about nationalism that garnered an enormous readership with the collapse of the Soviet Union and has since enjoyed a vibrant life in historical discussions. So what are the categories of history that are meaningful to Southeast Asians and Southeast Asianists? One way to work on an answer is through practices of research that juxtapose the scholar and the field of research in a traditionally distanced manner, separating "us" (the professional and scholarly researchers) from "them" (the subjects of study, wherever they are located in time and space). Another way is to engage in dialogues with people who tell stories about the past, whether orally, in scholarly texts, or works of fiction. We should do both. One part of the story of all humanity must surely be that we all tell stories.

Another World

Ajay Skaria

In his characteristically thought-provoking and wide-ranging essay, Joseph Miller has attempted nothing less than a reformulation of the terms on which world history is to be thought. He asks (if I may restate his argument): What is this "world" that world history is concerned with? Can another world be thought?

As Miller's essay suggests, this "world" is conventionally understood in terms of a movement from the particular or local to the general. As such, world history is concerned with those events that transcend the local to attain a wider or general significance. The conventional focus of world historians on state formation and diseases and germs that reshape continents is in keeping with this way of thinking about the world. Within this kind of world history, as Miller's argument suggests, Africa can only be marked by a lack, by a failure to attain significance.

I worry, however, that while he has very effectively pointed to the problems with the "world" as it is conventionally understood, he has not produced an effective or sufficient break with it. Here, I would like, first, to point out continuities in his essay with the older paradigm and, second, locate the precise ways in which Miller's essay breaks with that paradigm.

Let me begin with the continuities. When he proposes a multicentric approach to world history, he does so through a twofold argument: first, by pointing to the distinctiveness of Africa and, second, by locating the way in which, through this distinctiveness, Africans participated in world history no less than anyone else. To my mind, the first of these arguments is open to serious questioning, and the second is too preliminary.

From *Historically Speaking* 6 (November/December 2004)

Two convergences with conventional world history mark his argument about the distinctiveness of Africa. First, Miller locates the distinctiveness of Africa in its "communal ethos." As a historian of South Asia, I cannot claim any knowledge of Africa that would allow me to disagree with him. But what worries me nevertheless are the congruences between this description and conventional accounts of premodern societies generally. In conventional narratives, the premodern is the site of direct, face-to-face interaction, and the coming of modernity disrupts this communal ethos. To find these themes returning in Miller's attempt to identify a distinctively African logic—albeit with a twist where the traditional is no longer the site of ossified ranks but of multiple and proliferating identities—is somewhat disconcerting. Second, defining a culture as a shared commonality always excludes some who live within the culture but do not subscribe to its "ethos." This exclusive inclusion is justified by the method of generalization, which allows such particulars to be either excluded as unrepresentative or otherwise subsumed under the broader culture.

Miller's break from conventional world history is more marked in his attempt to think about the relation between Africa and the world in terms of dispersion. Thus the argument that Africa played an active role in modern world history. In this insistence on the productive role of dispersion, Miller breaks with the conventional subsuming of the particular within the general.

But this is a limited dispersion. "On the scale of world history, these dispersed, continentally specific strategies . . . were realizations of a single pan-Atlantic (and ultimately global) integrative economic process." Having introduced the theme of dispersion, the essay nevertheless at crucial points treats this dispersion not as constitutive but as integrated into a global process; it ultimately subordinates the dispersion to a totality. In this sense, the task of breaking with conventional world history, though so provocatively broached, remains incomplete. It seems to me that the stakes of making such a break are extremely high. For world history is not just a subfield of history. In its practice, what becomes evident is the otherwise not so apparent assumption of totality that marks the dominant paradigm of history.

An argument based on generalizing from particulars necessarily presumes a totality. Without such a totality, generalizing would be an unstable and even impossible exercise. To the world, there can be no outside, no context: the world is the context. To attempt a world history is also to attempt a total history.

To the extent that a work of history presumes such a totality, it is a world history, even if it limits its compass to a village or an individual. Consider, for instance, Carlo Ginzburg's riveting classic, *The Cheese and the Worms.* All the loving details with which the book renders Mennochio remain particulars to the extent that the book's argument claims a relation to a generality—if the details of Mennochio are important, as the book sometimes seems to suggest, it is because they are representative of the rural world of that time and place.

What then would be another history, a history that refuses totality? Intimations of such a history abound in the practice of historians. Consider the term *context,* affirmed over and again in the work of historians. At work potentially in this term *context*—"never absolutely determinable, never saturated" (Jacques Derrida, "Signature Event Context," *Margins of Philosophy*)— is a constant deferral that threatens totality and makes it impossible. When Miller questions world history and affirms multicentric histories, he does so partially by insisting on "history's core emphasis on change arising from contingency and complexity . . . history's distinctive reasoning from context." Similarly, Ginzburg's book is never the total history that it sometimes presents itself as; it produces a context that cannot be totalized through generality.

But despite historians' celebration of context, it is usually tethered in historical works to a concept of justice. The judge requires a totality so that different positions can be rendered comparable through measurement and evaluation. It might seem ill considered to describe today's historian as a judge; if anything, the problem might appear to be that historians suspend judgment even when confronted with obvious horrors. Yet the historical discipline cannot so easily abjure the role of the judge: it is required in establishing causal relations, in identifying the principal actors, and so on.

Some of these problems emerge in Ginzburg's recent book, *The Judge and the Historian,* where he argues that judges can make only limited use of context (as when insanity provides the context for a crime), since it leads not to established facts but only conjectures and possibilities; in contrast, he suggests, context is crucial in the most vital forms of historiography. Simultaneously Ginzburg points to the affinities between justice and context. Both share, as he puts it, the belief that it is possible to prove that X did Y. And context itself emerges only because of the absence of the facts that are required for proper judgment: context, he suggests, should be considered as an array of historically determined possibilities that serves to fill in what documents do not tell us. Here, context becomes a more labile form of judgment, a supplement to facts that softens their sharp edges. A consequence of his argument is that it disallows serious consideration of the way context potentially quite undoes justice, making impossible facts as we have usually understood them, complicating the belief that X did Y.

To consider these latter possibilities seriously is both to refuse judgment in the classical sense and simultaneously push beyond the lazy position that there are multiple contexts that are all in different ways valid. Consider Shahid Amin's *Event, Metaphor, Memory: Chauri Chaura, 1922–1992*. An eminent historian effectively expressed disappointment that the book had limited itself to providing local detail about the famous torching of a police station in 1922 that provided the occasion for Gandhi to call off the noncooperation movement. That historian, of course, had completely misunderstood the task undertaken by the book. For if it is local, it is not so in the sense of producing the world of the peasants of Chauri Chaura. Close to the beginning of the prologue, Amin writes: "In order not to write like the Judge, I have tried to find out how the Judge wrote." Involved here is the refusal of the world in a conventional sense: there can be no judgment that constitutes the world, whether it be the colonial, national, or local or microhistorical world.

But note that this is not a refusal of the world that celebrates myriad contexts, many worlds, and multiple centers. (Such celebration of multiplicity usually fails to recognize that the knowledge-practice of generality that produces the "world" is inseparable from domination and that this world cannot be simply replaced by multiplicity.) Rather, refusing subsumption within the world, *Event, Metaphor, Memory* nevertheless stays with the world but aporetically and interrogatively ("I have tried to find out how the Judge wrote"). Broached here is the thought of a constitutive dispersion *with* the world, a dispersion that can neither be integrated within one process nor be understood as a proliferation of multiplicity. This constitutive dispersion is that of marginality, where that which is subsumed within the generality of the world refuses such subsumption and, from and as the margin, questions the center. This questioning involves not multiple contexts but the thought of another justice—a justice that, affirming the margin, must interrogate the Judge.

Note also that Amin does not think of what he does as a radical break with historical practice. "Like other members of my tribe, I have in this book attempted to interrogate the interrogators." "Other members"—perhaps those who, refusing the logic of the tribe, have stayed with questions of marginality? For this insistence on a margin that refuses to be marginal is scarcely new, even if historical works have rarely attempted it as productively or in as sustained a manner as in *Event, Metaphor, Memory*. It is there in Ginzburg's attempt to derive the modern practice of history from biographical practice—with "history" understood as concerned with the state and "biography" as concerned with the adventurer, the failure, and the marginal figure. It is there Miller's insistence on "bringing Africa in on Africa's terms" and in his claim that tragedy may be the register of world history. Indeed, perhaps the very term *context,* when it is interrogated someday in a sustained manner, will be seen to have always provided intimations of the margin that refuses to be marginal.

Taking our cues from Amin, perhaps it could be said that another world history cannot only seek to produce a new "world" that is more balanced and inclusive of the margins. Rather, another world history will pose the question of the margin to the world and will constantly rend this world.

Africa in a Multicentric World History

Beyond Witches and Warlords

John K. Thornton

J oseph Miller has advised world historians that they would do well to pay
attention to Africa because its essential differences from the rest of the
world give it a special character that needs to be addressed in its own terms
and not in the older nineteenth-century language of history or anthropology.
As a longtime teacher of world history, I find this refreshing and absolutely
on the mark, since the observation of interregional differences is the soul of
comparative history, and it is ultimately as comparative history that world
history makes most sense to students and to the larger audiences we occasionally address.

It has made a difference to our understanding of world history to learn,
for example, that Africans lived in villages before they farmed in some areas
and farmed before they lived in villages in others, and it was thus the African
experience that caused us to rethink the nature of the Neolithic Revolution,
not just in Africa but everywhere. Some Africans further confounded conventional thinking by going from the Stone Age to the Steel Age without both-
ering in many areas to pass through a Bronze Age: Africans produced large
quantities of textiles without much machinery, bumper harvests without the
plow. Contemplating these challenges to the usual model of economic pro-
gression shakes our conceptions and leads us to a better understanding of
how we all came to be the way we are today. If African mercantile elites, like
the Juula of West Africa, managed to live in independent, self-governing
towns and to challenge rulers for political control, what does that mean for
the widespread discourse on the early modern world that looks for the origins
of the bourgeoisie in Western Europe and its nonemergence in various parts

of Asia as key components to the structure of the modern world? The Industrial Revolution in Europe led to the Trade Revolution in nineteenth-century Africa, a time when Africans abandoned much of their metallurgical and textile production for imports and began the massive export of largely agricultural goods, thus setting their course for underdevelopment. But they did so for perfectly rational reasons, defeating even the attempts of no small number of rulers and entrepreneurs to seek the introduction of machine production to the continent. This transformation—deindustrialization—which was well underway before any significant colonial presence, must lead us to reconsider deindustrialization in India's or Latin America's or China's abandonment of mechanized production in the fourteenth and fifteenth centuries. In short, presenting Africa's history as a counterexample, as another model, can do as much for our understanding of world history as Joseph Needham and Mark Elvin did by placing China back in the history of the early modern world as a dynamic actor and not simply as a static "Oriental Despotism."

Miller has warned us against seeing Africa as being too much like Europe and Asia. It is vital, he argues, to see Africans on their own terms, as measured by their own standards, which might not include states, monuments, or rulers. In order to achieve this African focus, Miller proposes that we reexamine what appear to be states in the coastal Atlantic area through the double imagery of warlords gathering followers and, at the same time, being limited by the discourse of witchcraft, for which there may be few comfortable European parallels. This radical reevaluation of African history, which breaks with a good deal of existing historiography, I find less satisfactory. In describing the founders of the early modern polities of Africa's Atlantic coast as "warlords," Miller presents them as ruthless gatherers of people and suggests that they were the cynical creators of impermanent polities. While certainly the founders of many of the states of coastal Africa might be described objectively as warlords, once the polity so founded passes a generation or so and gains institutional structure, the term is simply no longer applicable. None of the powerful states of the region—Benin, Asante, Dahomey, Kongo, or Matamba—can be described this way, for all possessed what we can easily see as the infrastructure of states: regularized taxation systems, judicial apparatuses, delineation of frontiers, systems of succession, delegation of authority, and chains of command.

It is easy to underestimate the structural complexity of Africa while overestimating the modernity of early modern Europe, the two errors compounding each other to create an artificially wide gulf between the two regions. If African state structures did not match ideal models of bureaucracies, neither did most other polities in the world, including those in early modern Europe, where orders were disobeyed, local enclaves of power held on against centralizing forces, taxes were avoided, and judicial decisions ignored. Distance, uncertainty of communication, and face-to-face connivances undermined the centralization of authority throughout the early modern world, and including Africa in the mix enriches, enlarges, and enhances our understanding of this phenomenon.

Because so many African societies did not leave written records of their own thoughts and motivations, we are hard pressed to know exactly how they thought and governed themselves. It is vital to try as best as we can with limited sources to understand what Africans thought they were doing as well as what literate observers, often outsiders with limited local experience, thought Africans were doing. Still, it is important to keep in mind the strong parallels with the rest of the world that keep Africa, for all its interesting local flavor, still very much a part of the familiar realities of power, economic rationality, and systematic thought.

The idiom of witchcraft, which Miller deploys as a tool to explain "the terms in which most people in Africa experienced the human exploitation of this era," still needs to be seen in its world historic context. The complex of beliefs and ideologies that we can label as "witchcraft" was an interesting and specifically African take on various theories of power ranging from the ideas expressed by Locke, Hobbes, and Rousseau in Europe to the theory of the "Third Rome" in Russia or the "Mandate of Heaven" and related Neo-Confucian political ideas for Chinese philosophers. In west-central Africa, for example, the idea of witchcraft, at least in the political as opposed to the private realm, was a two-part concept that included the idea of the "good king" as well as the "witch king." Good kings were virtuous rulers, and promises to look out for the poor, protect the weak, and serve the community were a regular part of the oaths that kings swore on their coronations. Their opposites were the wicked kings, who used the same powers both temporal and occult to enlarge their personal wealth and power and, thus, like the private merchants who might also participate in the occult as well as the material world, were suspect of witchcraft. The elaboration of these sorts of schemes, to the degree that they can be teased from original source material, is certainly an interesting twist on political theory and can help to illuminate other political theories advanced in other areas.

The rulers of the African polities that were regularly visited by slave traders were not necessarily just warlords personally enriching themselves and perhaps subject to witchcraft accusations for the unholy connivance with strangers. They might be important slavers and good rulers at the same time, at least in the eyes of their subjects. Queen Njinga of Matamba (r. 1624–63), an important participant in the slave trade, was both loved and feared for her alleged occult powers. Like many others, she regarded the taking of slaves as an integral part of warfare, and as long as her subjects accepted the basis for her wars, they could live with their consequences for the slave trade.

One might do well to conceive of the polities of Atlantic Africa as "fiscal-military states" much as the states of Western Europe were at the same time. Groups from within an area grasped at local resources or long-distance trade to negotiate with other powerful groups to enhance their power and to make war. European states engaged in nearly constant warfare and an equally constant search for the means to pay for it, and revolutions broke out when the two ran into each other.

African rulers managed to build larger and more centralized states through similar strategies, and the acquisition of slaves as dependents was one part of the equation, just as the sale of slaves to European merchants was another part. If the resources of America enabled kings of Spain, Portugal, France, and England to enhance their fiscal and military power, then the slave trade helped African rulers to increase their domestic power and expand their domains. And for them, too, revolution might be the result of too great a push and too big a distance between ambition and results, as the seductive combination of strategic designs and the means to pay for them through captives brought African rulers too deeply into the slave trading economy. When Beatriz Kimpa Vita accused the kings of Kongo indirectly of witchcraft in 1704 for failing to end wars and unite the country, she was expressing in the terms of the political philosophy prevalent at the time a revulsion for the particular sort of fiscal-military state that Kongo represented. However, this does not mean that other kings in other times who were regarded as "good kings" might not make war on their neighbors and enslave the captives, so long as the wars were regarded as necessary.

Miller clearly puts his finger on the point of greatest interest for world historians by focusing thus on the slave trade, for it is a great moral issue and also one that forces us to examine closely the complexities of African society and the state, touching as it does on conceptions of power and legitimacy and on the relationship between Africa and Europe. Once we go beyond seeing the slave trade as Europeans raiding the African coast (which rarely happened) or the workings of a simple "gun/slave cycle" in which African weaknesses were cynically manipulated by Europeans, we can begin to enter into a world of complex politics that raises not only questions intrinsic to the slave trade but also to the use of power in general.

Thus, though I question some of his specifics, I wholeheartedly endorse Miller's larger point that we ought to consider African dynamics as a part of world history to be placed alongside the history of other regions. Africa has its own unique political, ideological, and economic history. Adding it to the larger picture of world history will enrich our understanding of other areas with a different combination of circumstances and ideas.

Multicentrism in History

How and Why Perspectives Matter

Joseph C. Miller

In my initial essay I limited myself to exploring implications of giving Africa a place of its own in thinking historically about the world. But by analogy my argument applies to anyplace round the globe. For that matter, one might extend the general argument to the multiplicity of voices within any of the places that historians study conventionally. I will use my few words here to try to elaborate the broader implications of the points that I phrased in terms of Africa's particularities. I am well and happily aware—as Duchesne welcomes but as Skaria and others worry—that in doing so I affirm my perspective as a historian rooted in the modern discipline of the Western academy. That's how it is. We therefore might as well make the fact of perspective an opportunity rather than fret about it as a burden.

All history is someone's "our story," as I acknowledged in the *American Historical Review* address to which Duchesne refers. The debate in these pages is thus inevitably, but not defeatingly, limited. In this case, it comes down to a relatively parochial and academic discussion about Africa among scholars not raised in Africa, nor resident there, nor writing primarily for audiences living in African contexts. Collectively we evoke the spirit of the mostly North American community of world historians—scholars like myself who, in proclaiming the multiplicity of stories to be told in a balanced world history, presume to speak for others.

From the subaltern perspective, as Skaria reminds us, thinking of a world in these multiple terms risks essentializing one voice in the chorus, a singular abstracted *global* story that marginalizes personal, local, and regional experiences, and hence complementing perspectives. A world history of the dominating proportions that Skaria imagines would indeed marginalize, and that is why I share his reservations about the modern abstractions that characterize the usual practice of world history, including but not limited to "migrations," "religion," "economics," "environment," and "states." Throughout the Americas others thus also validly claim stories of Africa as theirs. Within the United States, parallel issues of perspective accompany the welcome development of Native American history. But Native Americans—no more than dominant historians—cannot claim monopolies on their stories. The principle of multiple perspectives that inheres in my notion of a multicentric world history demands the contributions of all to the "cacophony" that worries Manning but inspires Salman. Perspectives are at the heart of what historians are now taking seriously within the familiar confines of European and American history. They are essential parts of our stories as well as prominent parts of the stories of others, and historians won't get on with their job of understanding anyone until they learn to engage them all, at home and abroad.

To make my point about multiplicity, I must (self-reflexively) create an imagined "Africa" by focusing selectively on "African" motivations that strike me as distinct from ours. How, some of my respondents here wonder, can I—or any outsider—have any insights into past African experiences? I, of course, rely on Africans' historical behavior, as well as their own expressive arts (verbal, plastic, kinetic), particularly the ones that initially baffle me. So confusion, the ability to wonder, is the first step on the road toward understanding. Persistent outsiders like me can eventually learn enough of others' ways of thinking and enter sufficiently into their collective awareness to articulate their worlds revealingly—if primarily to other outsiders. Americans writing the history of France do this all the time. Multiple perspectives are additive, not competitive. Or, as Skaria would put it, collectively they approach "truth" (although I would say "understanding"). On larger scales, this outsider's privilege is by definition also the valid perspective of the world historian.

A phrase familiar to anthropologists and to anyone who has recognized the "otherness" amidst which we all live alludes wryly to this multiplicity of perspectives as "working misunderstandings." I would now qualify my entire professional experience as forging productively working misunderstandings with the people in the past whom I have studied. I would thus strengthen Reynolds's tentative observation that "sometimes things that seem obvious are also misleading": to me, everything that seems obvious is therefore misleading.

Unlike Skaria, I do not find "context" theoretically elusive or somehow diminishing of one's own subjectivity: for historians, it is not a theoretical issue but rather a pragmatic one of sensing the circumstances that actors saw as meaningful, or the meanings they sensed in the circumstances we observe. We create meaningfully coherent stories by focusing on a tiny minority of the potentially perceptible aspects of a situation.

The other operative term in my phrasing of multiplicity is "engaged." Engaged humans construct the terms of their engagements cognitively, thus culturally, selectively, and historically. Since identity and survival are at stake, these selective perceptions of others are spontaneous, often emotional, and always political. That is: cultures, those inherited, imagined identities, are survival as we know it. Engagements beyond ourselves are important to historians because they inherently motivate change, as the McNeills famously realize elsewhere.

What strikes me as the distinctive opportunity for world historians, then, is to understand all the parties engaged, each on distinctive terms of their own, independently of the behaviorialist abstractions (e.g. economics, sociology) that may also describe what they did in terms less organically related to what they thought they were doing. The neglect of the experienced self is a violation of dignity, which South Asian historians, cited here by Skaria, have protested from subaltern perspectives. The modern Western abstractions they resist miss the supple ways in which others (and ourselves, for that matter) get on with business, sex, war, and all the other rich experiences of life.

The "others" thus imagined are therefore always historical, constructed at moments in time and space out of immediate contexts of engagement. In my original essay I contrasted an African communal ethos with Western individualism. I suppose I could further contrast Descartes' *cogito ergo sum* with Africans' equally philosophical "I belong, therefore I am." Since collective self-reliance is the strategy of the disadvantaged in all historical contexts, in Africa people may therefore have accented what I call a "communal ethos" in reaction to the individuating challenges of the commercial contexts in which they found themselves increasingly immersed.

The singular "Africa" I evoked is specific to the question I raised about Africa's place in world history. If I had been writing for my Africanist colleagues, who found my homogenizing phrasing particularly dangerous, I would have risked losing the rest of our readers in the intricacies of matrilineal descent or Lunda/Ruund or "trading diaspora." By identifying Africans as subscribing to a communal ethos, I neither deny parallel tendencies among ourselves nor imply that collective consciousness did not prevail elsewhere in the past. Thornton thus exaggerates the extent of the intended contrast; Africans no more "abandon[ed] individualism" (presuming that they had once had it?) than we also lack intensely collective loyalties. For Africans the communal ethos *contains* individual tendencies; they resent presumed intimates taking advantage of them, just as we value (and routinely violate) generosity and loyalty within families. Understood as intended, my emphasis on a communal ethos usefully demonstrates, I continue to think, my point about multiple and selective perspectives on the human experiences that we all share.

For years now, Thornton and I have been happily debating the relevance of states to understanding Africa's past. Thornton's response here to my emphasis on the strong and local communal ethos in Africa enables me to restate the difference between us. Thornton stresses the "structures" (his word) that he sees as shaping early modern Africa history. I, on the other hand, highlight interpersonal relations and the particularities of Africans' responses to historical change. The same distinction applies in other historiographical contexts. Do historians study the conceptual complexities of "the imperial presidency" in the United States or the "constitutional monarchy" in England as givens, or do we take on the dynamics of the face-to-face encounters through the long series of specific contexts and multiple and contending perspectives that led politicians to create them and also to ignore them? To the extent that historians also indulge in the former, they consort with political philosophers. To the extent that the social sciences achieve generality (Skaria's term), they become abstract, hence relevant to us as historians only as means, not as our proper ends.

The responses assembled here interlock in ways that illustrate this accent on perspectives and collectives. The fundamental perspectival gulf among my respondents seems to divide those wary of diversity in the world from others who celebrate multiplicity and are therefore suspicious of global macronarratives. Diversity is sometimes more than faintly chaotic, and it's well worth wanting to unite humanity, given the derogation and divisiveness that stereotyped contrasts express. Unity appears benign to the dominant, but it is oppressive to those who experience uniting paradigms as alien. Manning thus worries about "cacophony" drowning out the sweet harmonies of abstractions; Salman, on the other hand, embraces existential "cacophony" as enrichingly harmonious rather than divisively discordant. All struggle with my use of *Africa* and *the world* to mark contrasts of the sort that, as Manning acknowledges, are utterly essential to human cognition, even basic identity (individual or collective), and thus to historical thinking. Differentiation, or perspective, is a first step in imposing order on the chaos of reality, present or past.

So we all have to draw contrasts. We risk essentializing only when we slide away into abstractions and theory as ends in themselves rather than using them instrumentally as a few among the many, all partial guides that historians pragmatically assemble to sense how and why responsive, engaged, supple people in the past did what they did. History, as I have said elsewhere, is not a science; it does not lead to the sort of generalizations that rightly worry Skaria. Reynolds attempts to balance the poles, or reverse the comparison, by using the modern global diaspora to portray the world as "African" as well as to place Africa squarely within "world" historical themes. Northrup deploys a parallel device, chiding Africanists for ignoring much of the world, a point that I endorse, although I would not differentiate historically relevant regions within Africa, as he does, in terms of their external connections. Thornton economically and provocatively also reverses the usual Western-based comparison across a range of eras and issues that I did not take up in my abbreviated illustration of the many parallels between "bourgeois" (in Thornton's European phrasing, equivalent to witchcraft in mine) Europe and eighteenth-century Atlantic Africa. What does this "African" perspective tell us about ourselves? How different is it from Marx's materialist formulation of the "communal ethos" as "class solidarity" and capitalism as ravenously consumptive of "labor"?

This basic and valuable and multiple perspectivity of history led me deliberately to select the slave trade to illustrate my broader argument. Atlantic slaving is likely to seem familiar to, and also (and therefore) to be widely misperceived among, my readers. On the other hand, West Africans experienced the era as one of collectively risky but personally opportune acquisition of valuable imports from alien and therefore irrelevant merchants. Similarly rhetorical strategies led me to refer to "witches" and "warlords," because both terms are emotionally loaded buzzwords for Americans—things *we* would *never* be. Africans and other historians in mnemonic environments know that one achieves memorability by telling their stories in the most surprising, most (initially) unbelievable manner possible. It would have taken at least a book to present the immediate implications of multicentrality by trying to explain any of the less-dramatic aspects of Africa's rich and varied past.

World history should rest on the same epistemological principles as any other sort of history. "World" history differs only in applying these to any contextualization (a logical polar contrast with abstraction) longer in time-scale and broader in space than what the actors involved took into account.

This concrete, actively engaged, subjective *contextualization* is unsullied by the neutral, nonperspectival, abstractions that Skaria accurately senses in conventional world history.

It follows from this definition of world history, as McNeill observes in other terms, that historical actors cannot give direct evidence of the processes and patterns that world historians distinctively can elicit. World historians—like historians working on smaller scales—can deploy the broader and longer perspectives they develop to illuminate short-term and local outcomes inexplicable to the actors, accounting for factors that would otherwise appear as dei ex machina, revealing ironies and innocence and ignorance, even explaining (however sadly) otherwise unthinkable tragedies, like the Atlantic commerce in enslaved people.

From the African communal ethos emerged what in my more structuralist days I once termed a "political economy of people" in which Africans struggled to assemble as many and as great a variety of personal connections as they could—ideally ones of respectable dependency but if necessary the humiliating abject dependency of enslavement. Faced with the variety and quantity of imports that the Atlantic trade provided, powerful Africans exchanged people, dependents of their rivals when they could get away with it, for goods, which in turn they used to claim more people for themselves, particularly women.

Europeans, on the other hand, were operating under the short-term pressures of an overwhelmingly rapid capitalist expansion throughout the Atlantic, borrowing more than they could pay back, in the expectation of expanding their operations to generate adequate returns in the future. In turn, they loaned these goods to African suppliers to generate eventual payments in captive humans. But African and European (or collective and individual) perspectives on the timing of "eventual" differed. Market swings and creditors forced European slavers to demand more people sooner than Africans anticipated, in satisfaction of the debts in Africa that they had stimulated. Europeans wanted to buy male laborers, and Africans wanted to retain fertile females. But, against the wishes of both parties, 35 percent–40 percent of those sold into the Atlantic slave trade were women. No one, on either side, planned that.

My Africanist colleagues would urge me to add that these processes eventually drove most of the involved parties within Africa to exploit one another. Were Europeanists represented in this forum, they would add that similar circumstances in the Atlantic led Europeans to mutual exploitation as well. The terms of engagements in world history thus differ from those in conventional

history, with the implication—no doubt startling to some who apply generalizations indiscriminately—that exploitation occurs more within (where values are nominally shared) than between autonomous groups with differing
values, in this case Africans and Europeans.

Multiple centers offer selectively coherent perspectives, and they are often
many indeed, particularly over longer terms and on larger scales. However,
world history also lurks in the background of even the most parochial of historical problems; in fact, the greater the parochialism, or the more local the
focus, the more immediately loom broader contexts of which actors are effectively unaware or do not take into account, usually to their frustration and
bafflement, or worse. Thus, to keep to the examples within the framework
featured in this forum, in Africa circumstances and considerations utterly
unknown to American planters and only dimly visible to even the most experienced and perspicacious European slavers on the African coast significantly
conditioned the assemblage of enslaved workforces in the New World. Similarly within Africa, local communities purged themselves of "witches" to deal
with pan-Atlantic and global processes evident to them only as betrayal from
within.

So strong were these internal perspectives, in at least some cases in Africa,
that these engagements were not perceived as "painful encounters" with others (McNeill). I indicated as much with my original remark about purging
the body politic of its corrupting components; applying the point to Thornton's "good kings," people tolerated, even welcomed, their military and fiscal
demands because they understood them as purging the polity—that is, themselves—of the treasonous within by selling "witches" to merchants (themselves suspected of similar tendencies). African occult defenses domesticated
and disabled the firearms of the Europeans, so far as they could tell, since failure flowed from incompetent or unfaithful manipulation rather than flawed
devices. Europeans struggled to control the bodies of those they enslaved but
not their spirits, the captives' true connections to their separate worlds.

If world history extends the conventional epistemology of the discipline,
it does so be centering on multiplicity of perspectives. Conventional history
has always worked *within* a single perspectival framework; all others were
"people without history" or living enveloped in what we could perceive only
as myth, as Salman says. Historians could thus presume that the authors of
written sources knew what they were talking about and engaged their corre-
spondents on shared cultural terms. But world historians cannot.

I am commenting on two dynamics of world history: (1) the ways in
which people act in historical contexts visible a posteriori to the historian but

not to the actors themselves. One can thus properly study small villages in Africa or in medieval Italy in their world historical contexts. "Atlanticization" of American history is currently moving strongly toward contextualization of this sort. In other contexts I prod Americanists to extend this strategy to "Africanize" their colonial era as well. World history may also study (2) how people systematically engage one another across the boundaries between their multiple, internally autonomous perspectives, as both—or all—sides reinvent themselves in contact with perfectly ordinary people whom, as strangers, they must construct as "others."

An awareness of the multiplicity of perspectives inherent in all history must mark the future of the profession. The sphere of unperceived chaos somewhere "out there" is vanishing. We are all becoming neighbors. Fewer and fewer "great unknowns" thus remain, and the frustrations of failure are visited more intensely, and at greater removes, on the "others" to whom we are growing close enough to demonize. Perhaps the resulting agonies are merely growing pains. But most people live too close to the edge to have the space in which to embrace difference with any confidence. Even so, "our story" must now incorporate everyone's stories. As McNeill says, world history provokes us to think more deeply about ourselves.

African Encounters

David Northrup

A s I rode in a crowded jitney bus in rural Nigeria in 1966, the old woman sitting next to me wet her fingertip, rubbed it gently on my arm, and then scrutinized it to see if any color had come off my pale skin. That memory came rushing back years later as I read an account of some Africans' reactions to the first European visitor to the Senegal River in 1455: "some . . . rubbed me with their spittle to discover whether my whiteness was dye or flesh." A Ugandan colleague who studied in Switzerland tells the story of a bold little girl in that country who performed the same experiment on him and reported to her schoolmates that he was "black but not sooty."

History is a dialogue between the present and the past, as well as an exercise in cross-cultural understanding. What we bring to the inquiry influences what we discover, and what we discover may reshape our understanding of our own time and place. Sometimes, as in the case of the wet-finger test, we find a common humanity that transcends time and culture, but often it is a struggle to bridge the gap between our expectations and the historical evidence we uncover.

My decision to become a historian of Africa was very much a product of my own life and times. I had gone to newly independent Nigeria as a Peace Corps volunteer, and my many fascinating experiences there moved me to study it when I returned. I was not alone. The field of African history itself had arisen in tandem with the independence movements in African colonies in the late 1950s and early 1960s and in sympathy with their aspirations. Like other Africanists of my generation, I wanted to discover the "real" Africa that lay beyond older narratives' focus on European explorers, merchants, missionaries, and empire builders. The term *Afrocentric* didn't yet exist, but it

From *Historically Speaking* 6 (November/December 2004)

describes our interest in bringing to light the historic antecedents of the proud African achievers of the present. Our enthusiasm may have led to exaggerations, but our desire to dislodge old paradigms forced us to base our studies on solid research and to pursue the implications of Africa-centered history to new levels. Despite blind spots and biases, recent scholars have made solid advances in understanding the African past.

The new African history has influenced scholars reexamining Atlantic history and added the names of African states and rulers to the textbooks, but it has also had to contend with other revisions of African history coming from historians of Europe and the Americas. Especially in versions intended for popular audiences, these accounts sometimes seemed to turn the old Eurocentric narrative of Africa on its head. In place of European heroes saving Africa, a new generation of anticolonial historians presented European villains bringing exploitation, underdevelopment, conquest, and cultural imperialism. Even though their new narratives were a much-needed corrective, their Eurocentricism tended to relegate Africans to being largely silent, generally hapless victims of the all-powerful Western world.

Was it possible to construct a more balanced narrative? I struggled with these issues while reexamining the encounters between Africans and Europeans during the four centuries before the imperial conquests of the late nineteenth century. A better narrative was needed to use the new Africanist scholarship to show how Africans understood and shaped these encounters. To make African perspectives vital and valid, I combed the records for historical voices that might be included. As *Africa's Discovery of Europe, 1450–1850*[1] moved toward completion, these voices from the past reshaped the narrative in unexpected ways.

For one thing, there proved to be a lot of African voices. One effect of the encounter with Europe was that many Africans learned European languages well enough to voice opinions that were recorded by Europeans, and some Africans wrote down their own views. Though it was not in my initial plan, the longest chapter in the book came to be about the many Africans in eighteenth- and early nineteenth-century Europe. But the most significant impact of these African voices was to broaden and deepen the exploration of many topics. African voices took the narrative to places that authorial caution, discretion, and concern for the sensibilities of readers and reviewers might have feared to go on its own. Among these were religion, slavery, and racism, often blended in intriguing ways.

For example, a letter from King Afonso I of the kingdom of Kongo to the king of Portugal in 1526 is commonly quoted for its chilling description of the destructive effects of the slave trade. But Afonso's request that his kingdom's trade with Portugal be restricted to "no more than some priests and a few people to teach in the schools, and no other goods except wine and flour for the holy sacrament" is less often noted, for our skeptical and secular age resists the clear implication that contacts with Europe included some Africans' sincere acceptance of Christianity. Nor is it commonly acknowledged that King Afonso's opposition to the slave trade centered on the fact that he has unable to stop many of his subordinate chiefs from selling fellow Kongolese in their desire to obtain the goods the Portuguese merchants brought. However, when Afonso himself had a great many captives from foreign wars to sell in 1540, his opposition to the slave trade vanished. He wrote that no ruler in Atlantic Africa "esteems the Portuguese goods so much . . . as we do. We favor their trade, sustain it, open markets [for it]." How widely Afonso deserves to be cited as a spokesperson for Africans may justly be debated, but one can hardly defend citing him so selectively that it distorts his views.

Though few wrote it down in so many words, other African rulers were as eager as Afonso for the goods the Atlantic trade brought, and many were more adept than he in reaping the profits of the trade from their equally eager European counterparts. For example, the royal merchants of the kingdom of Benin in 1724 rebuffed Dutch traders who had tried to convince them to pay higher prices for the goods they imported because costs had risen in Europe. The Benin officials asserted that the price in Europe "does not concern them" and insisted that valuations agreed upon in earlier years continue in force. Unable to make a profit, the Dutch eventually withdrew from Benin, but English traders eagerly took their place. One can argue that Europeans' command of the seas and colonial America gave them the upper hand in the Atlantic economy, but on the African coast they not only had to respect Africans' perceptions of prices; at Benin as elsewhere in West Africa, every European ship captain who came to trade also had to pay African officials hefty customs charges and fees and bestow rich gifts on local African officials. The European trading forts on the Gold Coast owed local rulers annual ground rents.

The fact that some coastal Africans participated willingly in the sale of slaves does not alter the injustice to those enslaved, but what should we make of African voices from that era who argued in favor of slavery? Jacob Capitein from the Gold Coast wrote his thesis on the theology of slavery at the University of Leiden in 1742. One of two eighteenth-century Africans to earn an advanced academic degree in Europe, he argued in elegant Latin that slavery was fully compatible with Christian theology and was often the means through which Africans became Christians. Though his case was based on European sources, Capitein's defense of slavery would not have seemed odd to many of his countrymen on the Gold Coast. In 1820, for example, King Osie Bonsu of the powerful state of Asante pressed a representative of the British government to explain why his people had turned against the slave trade, asking, "If they think it bad now, why did they think it good before? Is not your [Christian] law an old law, the same as the [Islamic] law?" He denied the slave trade was bad for his kingdom or that it increased the frequency of war. Rather, he argued, he made war for honorable reasons, and the gold and prisoners he took were his to keep or sell.

Capitein's thesis contains a second argument that, on first reading, seems even more surprising. Far from trying to curry favor with his hosts, Capitein was concerned that his thesis would upset his Dutch readers. He writes, "It is clear beyond doubt that most Netherlanders [believe] that Christian freedom cannot walk in step with slavery."[2] Although the enslavement of Africans had rich and powerful supporters in Europe, Capitein's words are a reminder that slavery had been banned in northern Europe for centuries and was unlikely to have much support among those not dependent on its profits. Before long the abolitionist movement would begin to tap popular antislavery sentiments, and some Africans were part of that movement in Europe. Forty-five years after Capitein issued his thesis, a dozen "sons of Africa" in Britain with a different view of Christian morality wrote a letter praising the British abolitionist Granville Sharp for his "long, valuable, and indefatigable labours . . . to rescue our suffering brethren in slavery" and to curb "the vicious violators of God's holy law."[3]

If African Christians could hold quite different positions on the morality of slavery, the presence of free, literate Africans—even advanced students and professors—in eighteenth-century Europe brings into question the common assumption that racial prejudices there were monolithic. Ignatius Sancho, one of the most notable of these African intellectuals, was well aware of the range of treatment an African might experience at European hands. Sancho was born on a slave ship in 1729 and lost his mother in infancy in Colombia. Yet when in 1766 he wrote to the English novelist Lawrence Sterne that "the early part of my life was rather unlucky," he was referring not to these hardships but to the lack of intellectually stimulating books. He had been brought to England at the age of two, where his own wit and good luck in time gained him employment and patronage from the Montagues, who had his portrait painted by Thomas Gainsborough. When he died in 1780, he was the first son of Africa to have an obituary in an English newspaper and the only one whose life was recorded in the *Dictionary of National Biography*. Sancho's fame was due less to his patrons, whose employment he left to become a humble shopkeeper, than to his literary achievements as a poet, playwright, musical theorist, and correspondent. His letters, published in two volumes after his death, are still in print.

Sancho's letters also attest to his awareness of the thin line that separated the social milieu where a black man of talent, manners, and morality might find honors and the one where racism reared its ugly head. He wrote to his fellow Afro-Briton Julius Soubise, who had been raised as a gentleman by the Duchess of Queensbury, contrasting their fortunate place in good society with "the miserable fate of almost all of our unfortunate colour" in slavery and warning of the contempt and "heart-racking abuse of the foolish vulgar" Soubise would face if he persisted in a life of debauchery.[4] Sancho's words might imply that the line between good treatment and bad was based on class, but the life story of another West African, Ukawsaw Gronniosaw, who made a humble living in England and the Netherlands after escaping slavery in Barbados, is full of the kindness and acceptance he received from the working poor and middle-class benefactors.[5]

Sancho was exceptional in that his wife was of African stock, but the many free African men who resided in eighteenth-century Europe were more likely to find brides from among the majority population. Gronniosaw married a poor English weaver named Betty, while other Africans married European women from higher social strata. The fact that such unions were tolerated does not imply that racist opposition did not exist. A letter signed by "Gustavus Vassa, the Ethiopian," printed in an English newspaper in 1788, was predicated on the notion that intermarriage was a prickly issue: "If the mind of a black man conceives the passion of love for a fair female, [is] he . . . to pine, languish, and even die, sooner than an intermarriage be allowed[?]"[6] The author, better known as Olaudah Equiano, the name he used in his autobiography, wedded the Englishwoman Susanna Cullen a few years later—without apparent incident. There is an interesting parallel between these marriages in Europe and those in coastal Africa in this era. Many European men resident there entered into long-term unions that seem as full of mutual love, mutual financial considerations, advantageous family ties, and beloved offspring as are common to the institution everywhere.

This brief overview can only hint at the value of looking at these early modern encounters through the eyes of contemporary Africans, even though the accounts that survive cannot be expected to represent the full range of experiences. Europeans and West Africans began their encounters with mutual curiosity about each other and an openness to the possibilities of continued relationships. African leaders were as capable as European ones of assessing what they might gain and were as eager to do so. To note that quite a number of coastal Africans found opportunities in the Atlantic trade for new wealth and power does not diminish the calamity of millions of other Africans being robbed of their freedom. Some Africans were also open to the cultural options in the encounters, including Christianity, literacy, and occasionally literary distinction in European languages. Appreciating the full range of the encounters enhances understanding not just of those precolonial centuries but also of the commercial and cultural changes that have continued long after the slave trade ended. If Africans are to appear on the stage of history as full human beings, then they must strut the boards as powerful partners as well as victims, as open to the opportunities the Atlantic brought as they were capable of suffering under its inequities.

NOTES

1. David Northrup, *Africa's Discovery of Europe, 1450–1850* (New York: Oxford University Press, 2002).

2. Jacobus Elisa Johannes Capitein, *The Agony of Asar: A Thesis on Slavery by the Former Slave,* trans. Grant Parker (Princeton, N.J.: Markus Wiener, 2001), 103.

3. Quoted in Olaudah Equiano, *The Interesting Narrative and Other Writings,* ed. Vincent Carretta (1789; repr., New York: Penguin Books, 1995), 326–27.

4. Ignatius Sancho, *Letters of the Late Ignatius Sancho, an African,* ed. Vincent Carretta (New York: Penguin Books, 1998), ix, xiv–xv, 46, 73.

5. Ignatius Sancho, *A Narrative of the Most Remarkable Particulars in the Life of James Albert Ukawsaw Gronniosaw, an African Prince, Related by Himself* (London, 1774).

6. Equiano, *Narrative,* 329.

PART 2

The Atlantic World

Only Connect

The Rise and Rise (and Fall?) of Atlantic History

Trevor Burnard

S tocks in Atlantic history are high. "We are all Atlanticists now," declares David Armitage with blithe disregard for the perils of hubris. The topic has developed the type of institutional apparatus that signals it is more than a passing fancy. Courses on "The Atlantic World" abound; positions in Atlantic history have been advertised at an increasing number of institutions; and postgraduate programs for Atlantic history specialists are now appearing. Atlantic historians gather at conferences at exotic locations around the world; research centers with an Atlantic focus are created every year; and funding opportunities to do Atlantic history are becoming more frequent. Perhaps most telling, major universities, research libraries, and scholarly organizations have begun to treat Atlantic history as a subfield, making it possible for a cadre of historians to advance their careers, meet lots of agreeable people who share their own predilections in interesting and stimulating places, and network through joint participation in seminars and fellowships.

The Atlantic way allows budding historians a multitude of new research and job opportunities. This is a remarkable turnabout, considering the dim prospects facing English-speaking historians of the early modern era in the late 1970s. For a graduate student in early American history, topics and areas that had previously been at the cutting edge of scholarship were now passé. The scholarship of the 1960s and 1970s led away from a broadening vision. The work of scholars influenced by the *Annales* school was extraordinary, ushering in a golden age of scholarship. But a major failure of social history in all its multitudinous varieties was a loss of focus. Historians concentrated

From *Historically Speaking* 7 (July/August 2006)

so intently on the detail of small-scale communities that, as Bernard Bailyn put it in an extremely influential 1982 jeremiad, previously "discrete and easily controllable" fields of knowledge had become "boundless" and "incomprehensible," the "wider boundaries" unclear. Historians coming into graduate school from the late 1970s into the mid-1980s were confronted by a bewildering number of studies of small-scale communities in early America, most of which were individually excellent but, taken together, generally led to confusion. To adapt the old joke told about either economists or lawyers, one could lay down side by side a host of community studies of New England towns and never come to an agreement.

Similarly, seventeenth-century British history was becoming ever more myopic, introspective, and irrelevant. Indeed scholars of the English Civil War undertook the discipline-destroying act of claiming that the object of their study—the English Revolution—did not really exist. It seemed as if there was nothing interesting left to be said about either early modern Britain or colonial America. Branching out into Atlantic history or the related New British History was a way of escaping intellectual stupefaction. It also gave aspiring academics an entrée into a still fiercely contested job market. In part, Atlantic history has developed out of the relentless need for scholarship to be about new and unexplored fields. In part, also, it has been an understandable response by historians—as attuned to market possibilities as any other group of professionals—to the changing market of academic scholarship and employment.

What I have said thus far may strike readers as unduly cynical in its emphasis on the career-enhancing potentialities of Atlantic history. But the institutional apparatus that has accompanied the advent of Atlantic history as one of the more important historiographical developments of recent times did not develop just because it met the needs of a generation of historians anxious to be established in a dynamic new area. Atlantic history has real intellectual clout. It has reinvigorated the histories of early America and Latin America. Its principal theme—that the Atlantic from the fifteenth century to the present was not just a physical fact but a particular zone of exchange and interchange, circulation, and transmission—is a conceptual leap forward. True believers in the approach argue that Atlantic history, with its emphasis on movement, fluidity, and connections between nations, peoples, and events, shows how the modern world was made. The idea of Atlantic history as a field of historical inquiry that is "additive," or more than the sum of an aggregation of several national or regional histories, pushes historians toward both methodological pluralism and expanded horizons. In short, my comments on the career-enhancing possibilities of Atlantic history may be cynical, but they are not the result of skepticism about the utility of Atlantic history as a method or as a subject of inquiry.

The language used to describe Atlantic history is revealing about its appeal. The words that come up most frequently when Atlantic history is described are "movement," "diversity," "complex," "networks," "creation," "negotiations," "enlargement," "dynamic," "permeable," "multiple," "invention," "exchanges," "broadening," and, above all else, "connections." By contrast, other types of histories are "narrow," "technical," "isolated," "domestic," and "static." I have listed them in this way, without attention to grammar, in order to capture the sort of ambience that modern politicians use to reflect the political and cultural tone of the post–cold war world.

For the aforementioned Bernard Bailyn, a leading proponent, the advantage of Atlantic history as a field is that it provides a way for historians, increasingly Balkanized into smaller and smaller subfields, to "put the story together again." Historians of the Atlantic world can talk about the "rise of the West" and the foundations of the modern world in a sophisticated fashion, one suitable for a contemporary audience convinced of the virtues of diversity and the reality of social and historical fluidity. For this reason, Bailyn stresses the roots of Atlantic history in a specific political moment in the history of the United States immediately following World War II. The idea of Atlantic history, he argues, came from a reformulation of Wilsonian universalism among Americanists of an internationalist mindset who concentrated on fostering links in an "Atlantic community" of countries with a common heritage of "Western Christendom." In the same way that Atlanticism provided a common focus for internationalists of that period, so now Atlantic history offers historians an escape from the self-defeating tendency to study smaller and smaller units unconnected with larger processes. Atlantic history allows historians to concentrate on the dynamic aspects of the past and become "narrators of worlds in motion—worlds as complex, as unpredictable, and as transient as our own."

For some historians, however, the motivation to do Atlantic history is very different. Many practitioners find attractive what critics of Atlantic history usually consider the greatest weakness of the field: the absorptive capacity of Atlantic history to soak up all manner of different kinds of concern into one very loosely interconnected system. Contra Bailyn, they do not want to put the story of the rise of the West back together again (even though some share Bailyn's concerns about lack of coherence). The last thing these Atlanticists want is a retreat into Eurocentrism, which seems like a new way of promoting imperialism without mentioning its name. Instead, they celebrate marginality rather than integration and focus on disaggregation as much as aggregation.

We can see these impulses at work in the reminiscences of Jack Greene about the origins of the first and most influential of Atlantic programs, the program in Atlantic History, Culture, and Society at the Johns Hopkins University. Greene was encouraged to found this program because of his seething discontent in the late 1960s about "the narrow Eurocentric" character of his institution. He was especially concerned with the lack of attention given to the black experience, which he knew was at least as important as the white experience in shaping the contours of early American life. He was determined to expand his department's geographical coverage into Third World areas, such as Africa and Latin America. Atlantic history was convenient shorthand to articulate this broadening of scope.

Greene was especially influenced by the work of the sociologist Edward Shils, who articulated in 1961 a distinction between centers and peripheries. What made Shils's work a valuable analytical tool was his emphasis on how authority between center and periphery had always to be negotiated rather than imposed. Moreover, authority did not always move from center to periphery but often travelled the other way around. As Greene saw it, center-periphery theory helped to demonstrate how peripheral areas could enjoy considerable autonomy and independence from the center.

One of the notable features of current Atlantic historiography is how much attention it gives to places like Providence Island near Nicaragua, Bance Island in West Africa, St. Eustatius, Nova Scotia, Barbados, and Vila Boa de Goias, near modern Brasilia. A criticism sometimes made about Atlantic history, usually muttered sotto voce at conferences, is that one of its purposes seems to be to find the most insignificant places and claim earth-shattering importance for them. In a lot of ways this unfair criticism is justified, because Atlantic historians argue that it is at the peripheries that the true lineaments of Atlantic history can be discerned. In small places, the impact of the collision between various worlds can be most clearly measured. If Atlantic history has a one-sentence credo, it is D. W. Meinig's contention that it comprises the study of "a sudden and harsh encounter between two old worlds that transformed both and integrated them into a single New World." The sum of the connections, Atlantic historians contend, is greater than the parts. David Hancock, for example, argues for what he calls a spider's-web approach in Atlantic history. He sees the Atlantic world as a complex, nonlinear, largely self-organizing system.

What, then, has been the impact of the "Atlantic turn" on historical study? In one area, the influence of Atlantic history has been undeniable. Early American history and Atlantic history have become almost synonymous. Early Americanists were always likely to be receptive to Atlantic history because of their tendency to see developments in colonial British America as bound to developments in Britain. It was a short step from being interested in the social and economic comparisons that could be made about Britain and colonial America to looking at what things connected the two areas and other societies on the various continents bordering the Atlantic Ocean.

Paradoxically, while the notion of bringing disparate continents together under the Atlantic rubric has breathed new life into the study of colonial America, it has also turned that field into something of a ghetto. The new focus on things Atlantic has led to significant disengagement between early American historians and early modern British historians. Such a sweeping statement needs to be qualified by acknowledging that in one important area, eighteenth-century British history, the historical connections between America and Britain have increased rather than decreased. The most-influential historians of eighteenth-century Britain—Linda Colley, Kathleen Wilson, J. C. D. Clark, John Brewer—have written important books on Britain that have an explicitly transatlantic focus.

Yet eighteenth-century British history has always been a less-crowded and less-influential field than that of the seventeenth century. There the decline of interest in American history among British historians has been palpable. In the heyday of the Cambridge Group for the History of Population and Social Structure, the linkages between the study of colonial British America and seventeenth-century England and Scotland were frequently made, to the extent that investigations into social structure in both Britain and America were part of a single project. These occur no longer. The disengagement has been particularly apparent on one side of the equation: English social historians no longer read the social history of the early colonies, even when it has direct implications for English social history. For example, James Horn's *Adapting to a New World: English Society in the Seventeenth-Century Chesapeake* has attracted virtually no attention among English social historians, despite its title, its extensive recreation of the social structure of the English West Country, and its enthusiastic reception by early American historians. Moreover, the leading journals in seventeenth-century British history show little to no interest in America. Journals with a broader ambit, such as *Past and Present* and the *Historical Journal,* ignore early America and the Atlantic world entirely.

Neither has the Atlantic world had much impact on U.S. history. Most work on early national and antebellum American history is resolutely focused on the history of America as a nation-state. As Joyce Chaplin argues, the best studies by mid-career historians of the Revolutionary period now tend to be about the early republic rather than the Revolution and are self-consciously indifferent to Atlantic perspectives. The field of the early republic, she suggests, exerts a gravitational pull on colonial American and Atlantic scholarship. Atlantic history not only fades the further we go beyond 1789 but comprises an ever-diminishing portion of the avalanche of scholarship produced by American historians of all time periods. Even the history of the American Revolution is not well integrated into the Atlantic world. Differing emphases of interpretation and approach now make colonial and Revolutionary American history almost two separate entities.

In sum, the response to Armitage's boast that "we are all Atlanticists now" must be "no, we are not." Some of us are Atlanticists, but many more historians, to whom Atlantic historians ought to feel a link, have no interest in the intellectual agenda set out by Atlantic historians. The relative lack of interest shown in Atlantic history by other historians should dampen our enthusiasm for making a whole-scale conversion to the delights of Atlantic history.

So, proceed with caution before jumping on the Atlantic-history bandwagon. It promises much as a field, but questions hover over whether it can deliver on that promise. For my generation of historians, the Atlantic-history movement has been a positive good, allowing us to travel to interesting places, meet like-minded people, and do work that is innovative and that does not replicate narrowly the work done by our social-history predecessors. The danger for the next generation of historians is what happens when the bar is raised, when work in Atlantic history has to be genuinely transatlantic, necessitating an in-depth knowledge of several cultures and several languages. Will early-American historians feel comfortable marooned from their compatriots who do United States history or early modern European history, and will they be happy being located in the institutional ghetto—fabulous as that ghetto may be—that contains Latin American, African, Asian, and world historians? In short, if you are part of the early-Americanist majority that keeps Atlantic history afloat, keep hold of your stocks in Atlantic history, but make sure you diversify sufficiently to avoid being hurt in the crash that follows a heady boom.

Does Equiano Still Matter?

Vincent Carretta

I have been invited to address the question of whether—despite the possibility that he fabricated his personal and African identities—the man best known today as Olaudah Equiano remains a central figure in the reconstruction of Atlantic history and to our understanding of the Atlantic world. Before I do so, let me briefly summarize his life, as he recounts it in his autobiography, and touch on the significant role he has played in historical and literary studies.

According to *The Interesting Narrative of the Life of Olaudah Equiano, or Gustavus Vassa, the African. Written by Himself* (London, 1789), Equiano was born in 1745 in what is now southeastern Nigeria. There, he says, he was enslaved at the age of eleven, and sold to English slave traders who took him on the Middle Passage to the West Indies. Within a few days, he tells us, he was taken to Virginia and sold to a local planter. After about a month in Virginia, he was purchased by Michael Henry Pascal, an officer in the British Royal Navy, who brought him to London. Pascal ironically renamed him Gustavus Vassa after the sixteenth-century Swedish monarch who liberated his people from Danish tyranny. During the eighteenth century, slaves were often given ironically inappropriate names of powerful historical figures like Caesar and Pompey to emphasize their subjugation to their masters' wills. With Pascal, Equiano saw military action on both sides of the Atlantic Ocean during the Seven Years' War. In 1762, at the end of the conflict, Pascal shocked Equiano by refusing to free him, selling him instead to the West Indies. Escaping the horrors of slavery in the sugar islands, Equiano managed to save enough money to buy his own freedom in 1766. In Central America he helped purchase slaves and supervised them on a plantation. Equiano set off on voyages of commerce and adventure to North America, the Mediterranean,

From *Historically Speaking* 7 (January/February 2006)

the West Indies, and the North Pole. Equiano was now a man of the Atlantic. A close encounter with death during his Arctic voyage forced him to recognize that he might be doomed to eternal damnation. He resolved his spiritual crisis by embracing Methodism in 1774. Later he became an outspoken opponent of the slave trade, first in his letters to newspapers and then in his autobiography. He married an Englishwoman in 1792, with whom he had two daughters. Thanks largely to profits from his publications, when Equiano died on March 31, 1797, he was probably the wealthiest and certainly the most famous person of African descent in the Atlantic world.

Over the past thirty-five years, historians, literary critics, and the general public have come to recognize the author of *The Interesting Narrative* as one of the most accomplished English-speaking writers of his age and unquestionably the most accomplished author of African descent. Several modern editions are now available of his autobiography. The literary status of *The Interesting Narrative* has been acknowledged by its inclusion in the Penguin Classics series. It is universally accepted as the fundamental text in the genre of the slave narrative. Excerpts from the book appear in every anthology and on any Web site covering American, African American, British, and Caribbean history and literature of the eighteenth century. The most frequently excerpted sections are the early chapters on his life in Africa and his experience on the Middle Passage crossing the Atlantic to America. Indeed it is difficult to think of any historical account of the Middle Passage that does not quote his eyewitness description of its horrors as primary evidence. Interest in Equiano has not been restricted to academia. He has been the subject of television shows, films, comic books, and books written for children. The story of Equiano's life is part of African, African American, Anglo-American, African British, and African Caribbean popular culture. Equiano is also the subject of a biography published in 1998 by James Walvin, an eminent historian of slavery and the slave trade.

Since the early 1970s we have witnessed a renaissance of interest in Equiano's autobiography and its author. During Equiano's own lifetime, *The Interesting Narrative* went through an impressive nine editions. Most books published during the eighteenth century never saw a second edition. A few more editions of his book appeared, in altered and often abridged form, during the twenty years after his death in 1797. Thereafter, he was briefly cited and sometimes quoted by British and American opponents of slavery throughout the first half of the nineteenth century. He was still well enough known publicly that he was identified in 1857 as "Gustavus Vassa the African" on the newly discovered gravestone of his only child who survived to adulthood. But after 1857 Equiano and his *Interesting Narrative* seem to have been almost completely forgotten on both sides of the Atlantic for more than a century. A notable exception was W. E. B. Du Bois, who in 1913 recognized Equiano's autobiography as "the beginning of that long series of personal appeals of which Booker T. Washington's *Up from Slavery* is the latest."[1] The declining interest in the author and his book is probably explained by the shift in emphasis from the abolition of the British-dominated transatlantic slave trade to the abolition of slavery, particularly in the United States, following the outlawing of the transatlantic trade in 1807.

The twentieth-century recovery of the man and his work began with the publication in 1969 by Paul Edwards of a facsimile edition of *The Interesting Narrative*. I have been teaching and researching Equiano since the early 1990s. Although I had heard of Equiano before then, I had never seen a copy of his work, and from what I had read about it, I assumed that it was a text more appropriate for American literature courses than for the British courses I was teaching at the time. Placing Equiano in the tradition of American autobiographical writing exemplified by Benjamin Franklin went unchallenged. They were both seen as self-made men who raised themselves by their own exertions from obscurity and poverty. No one thought to point out that since the publication in London of Equiano's autobiography preceded by decades that of Franklin's in the United States, rather than considering Equiano an African American Franklin, we would more accurately call Franklin an Anglo-American Equiano.

Preparing to teach *The Interesting Narrative* and later editing the text for Penguin Putnam, I began a series of discoveries that led to my decision to write a biography of its author. Many of those discoveries were ones I never expected, indeed, never wanted to make because they so profoundly challenged my sense of who Olaudah Equiano, or Gustavus Vassa, the African, was. Recent biographical discoveries cast doubt on Equiano's story of his birth and early years. The available evidence suggests that the author of *The Interesting Narrative* may have invented rather than reclaimed an African identity. If so, Equiano's literary achievements have been vastly underestimated. Baptismal and naval records say that he was born in South Carolina around 1747. If they are accurate, he invented his African childhood and his much-quoted account of the Middle Passage on a slave ship.[2] Other newly found evidence proves that Equiano first came to England years earlier than he says. He was clearly willing to manipulate at least some of the details of his life. Problematic as such evidence may be, any would-be biographer must now take it into account.

Reasonable doubt raised by the recent biographical discoveries inclines me to believe that the accounts of Africa and the Middle Passage in *The Interesting Narrative* were constructed—and carefully so—rather than actually experienced and that the author probably invented an African identity. But we must remember that reasonable doubt is not the same as conviction. We will probably never *know* the truth about the author's birth and upbringing. The burden of proof, however, is now on those who believe that *The Interesting Narrative* is a historically accurate piece of nonfiction. Anyone who still contends that Equiano's account of the early years of his life is authentic is obligated to account for the powerful conflicting evidence. And we must consequently reassess the ways in which we have interpreted and used his autobiography.

Equiano was certainly African by descent. The circumstantial evidence that Equiano was also African American by birth and African British by choice is compelling but not absolutely conclusive. Supporting Equiano's claim of an African birth, Adam Hochschild argues, is "the long and fascinating history of autobiographies that distort or exaggerate the truth . . . . But in each of these cases, the lies and inventions pervade the entire book. Seldom is one crucial portion of a memoir totally fabricated and the remainder scrupulously accurate; among autobiographers, as with other writers, both dissemblers and truth-tellers tend to be consistent."[3] A writer as skillful and careful as Equiano, however, could have been one of the rare exceptions that Hochschild acknowledges exist. Equiano certainly knew that to do well financially by doing good for the abolitionist cause, he needed to establish and maintain his credibility as an eyewitness to the evils of the transatlantic slave trade and slavery in its various eighteenth-century forms. He also knew what parts of his story could be corroborated by others and, more important, if he was combining fiction with fact, what parts could not easily be contradicted.

Why might Equiano have created an African nativity and disguised an American birth? The timing of the publication of *The Interesting Narrative* was no accident. Mainly through the efforts of the philanthropist Thomas Clarkson, the organized opposition to the African slave trade gathered and published evidence against the infamous practice from 1787 on. But before 1789 the evidence and arguments against the slave trade came from white voices alone. The only published black witnesses were clearly fictitious, found, for example, in the poems of Hannah More and William Cowper. In *An Essay on the Slavery and Commerce of the Human Species,* Equiano's future subscriber Clarkson acknowledged the desirability of hearing the victim's point of view. Clarkson dramatized the transatlantic slave trade by placing the trade in "the clearest, and most conspicuous point of view." Employing the virtual reality of fiction to convey factual experience, he imagined himself interviewing a "melancholy African." "We shall," he wrote, "throw a considerable part of our information on this head into the form of a narrative: we shall suppose ourselves, in short, on the continent of Africa, and relate a scene, which, from its agreement with unquestionable facts, might not unreasonably be presumed to have been presented to our view, had we really been there."[4] Initially, not even black opponents of the trade recognized the rhetorical power an authentic African voice could wield in the struggle. When Equiano's friend, collaborator, and future subscriber Quobna Ottobah Cugoano published *Thoughts and Sentiments on the Evil and Wicked Traffic of the Slavery and Commerce of the Human Species* in London in 1787, he chose not to describe Africa or the Middle Passage in much detail. A member of the Fante people from the area of present-day Ghana who had been kidnapped into slavery around 1770, Cugoano believed that "it would be needless to give a description of all the horrible scenes which we saw, and the base treatment which we met with in this dreadful captive situation, as the similar cases of thousands, which suffer by this infernal traffic, are well known."[5]

Equiano knew that what the antislave trade movement needed most in 1789 to continue its increasing momentum was the rhetorical power an authentic African voice could wield in the struggle. His autobiography corroborated and even explicitly drew upon earlier reports of Africa and the trade by some white observers and challenged those of others. His account of Africa is a combination of printed sources, memory, and imagination. Equiano appreciated that "only something so particular as a single life . . . could capture the multiplicity of . . . lives" in the eighteenth-century Atlantic world.[6] The abolitionist movement required precisely the kind of account of Africa and the Middle Passage that he, and perhaps only he, could supply. An African, not an African American, voice was what was needed. He gave a voice to the millions of people forcibly taken from Africa and brought to the Americas as slaves. Equiano recognized a way to do very well financially by doing a great deal of good in supplying that much-needed voice.

By forging a part of his personal identity and creating an Igbo national identity *avant la lettre,* Equiano became an effective spokesperson for his fellow diasporan Africans. As the Nobel laureate Nigerian author Chinua Achebe has observed, the consciousness of the Igbo identity that Equiano asserts is a far more recent phenomenon: "In my area, historically, [the Igbo people] did not see themselves as Igbo. They saw themselves as people from this village or that village. In fact in some places 'Igbo' was a word of abuse; they were the 'other' people, down in the bush. And yet, after the experience of the Biafran War, during a period of two years [1967–70], it became a very powerful consciousness. But it was *real* all the time. They all spoke the same language, called 'Igbo,' even though they were not using that identity in any way. But the moment came when this identity became very very powerful . . . and over a very short period."[7]

Contemporary scholars value Equiano's "unique first-hand account of eighteenth-century Igboland" so highly because so little other direct information about the mid-eighteenth-century Igbo exists.[8] But this same absence of evidence gave Equiano the opportunity for invention he needed if he was born in South Carolina rather than Africa. Equiano uses his autobiography to practice nation-formation as well as self-creation. He was a pioneer in the forging of an Igbo national identity.

To be sure, an argument has been made that an Igbo national identity was developing during the eighteenth century, but even if such an identity had been established by the time Equiano was writing, it was not the primary identity a native West African would likely have claimed, except possibly to outsiders.[9] During the eighteenth century the now more familiar national sense of Igbo was the result of the involuntary African diaspora: "A sense of pan-Igbo identity came only when its people left Igboland—an experience first imposed by the slave trade."[10] Whites used the term *Eboe* or *Igbo* in the diasporan sense throughout the eighteenth century. Like the terms *Guinea* and *Koromantyn, Eboe* was a geographical and supraethnic concept Europeans created that elided the significant cultural differences among various ethnic groups in West Africa.

Equiano speaks with the voice of an Igbo protonationalist proud of his homeland, no doubt aware that if he could rehabilitate the reputation of the Igbo in particular, he would rehabilitate the reputation of Africans in general. Equiano knew that earlier and contemporaneous commentators disagreed with his positive assessment of the peoples Europeans called Igbos, the slaves least desired by planters in the British colonies.[11] As one historian points out, "No Chesapeake planter is known to have expressed a preference for laborers originating in the Bight of Biafra, and indeed Ibo . . . slaves were held in particularly low esteem in much of the Caribbean and in South Carolina."[12] Scholars who overemphasize the few times Equiano uses the term *Eboe* often ignore the way he organizes his account of Africa. He moves from recollections about "Eboe" specifically to comments about Africans in general, and he closes his first chapter with a series of rhetorical questions that force his readers to draw conclusions about the universal nature of humankind from the evidence he has presented. Despite claiming to describe distinctively Igbo manners, he conflates accounts of various African ethnic groups to construct a kind of pan-African identity, a sort of essential African.

Modern scholars rightly point out that of the surviving brief eighteenth-century descriptions of the kingdom of Benin, Equiano's account of Igboland is the most fully developed. Equiano's description is certainly the most complete eighteenth-century ethnography of "Eboe" we have from a person of African descent and the only one not mediated by a white translator or transcriber. But critics and scholars have increasingly come to recognize that his account's apparent uniqueness does not guarantee its authenticity.[13] All that we know of Olaudah Equiano's existence in Africa comes from his own account, and that account was clearly intended to be part of the dialogue about the African slave trade. His representation of Igboland challenged competing images of a land of savagery, idolatry, cannibalism, indolence, and social disorder. If Equiano forged both his personal and national African identities, he risked being exposed as an imposter, thus discrediting the abolitionist cause, but the financial and rhetorical success of his book demonstrated that it was a risk well worth taking.

Every autobiography is an act of re-creation, and autobiographers are not under oath when they are reconstructing their lives. Furthermore, an autobiography is an act of rhetoric. That is, any autobiography is designed to influence the reader's impression of its author and often, as in the case of *The Interesting Narrative,* to affect the reader's beliefs or actions as well. The most constant quality of Equiano's *self* was his ability to transform himself, to redefine and refashion his identity in response to changing circumstances.

A manumitted (freed) slave faced a greater opportunity for redefinition than any other autobiographer. Manumission necessitated redefinition. The profoundest possible transformation was the one any slave underwent when freed, moving from the legal status of property to that of person, from commodity to human being. Former slaves were also immediately compelled to redefine themselves by choosing a name. Choosing not to choose was not an option. With freedom came the obligation to forge a new identity, whether by creating one out of the personal qualities and opportunities at hand or by counterfeiting one. Equiano may have done both. In one sense, the world lay all before the former slave, who as property had been a person without a country or a legal personal identity. Equiano's restlessness and apparent wanderlust once he was free may have been the result of his quest for an identity and a place in the world.

In the sense of raising himself from poverty and obscurity, Equiano was a more self-made man than Franklin, and he was as successful during his lifetime as Franklin in marketing that image of himself. Through a combination of talent, opportunity, and determination, Equiano became the first successful professional black writer. Franklin rose from poverty to prosperity; Equiano rose from being property in the eyes of the law to being the wealthiest person of African descent in Britain. Like Franklin, Equiano offered his own life as a model for others to follow. Equiano's personal conversions and transformations from enslaved to free, pagan to Christian, and proslavery to abolitionist, anticipated the changes he hoped to make in his readers, as well as the transformation he called for in the relationship between Britain and Africa. Equiano was an even more profoundly self-made man than Franklin if he invented an identity to suit the times.

Whether or not Equiano engaged in self-invention, attempts to pin him down to simply either an African, an American, or a British identity are doomed to failure. Once he was free, Equiano judged parts of North America reasonably nice places to visit, but he never revealed any interest in voluntarily living there. By Equiano's account, the amount of time he spent in North America during his life could be measured in months, not years. Whether he spent a few months, as he claims, or several years, as other evidence suggests, living in mainland North America, he spent far more time at sea. He spent at least ten years on the Atlantic Ocean and Mediterranean Sea during periods of war and peace between 1754 and 1785. The places he considered as a permanent home were Britain, Turkey, and Africa. Ultimately he chose Britain, in part because Africa was denied him, despite his several attempts to get there.

As we all do, Equiano chose from the various subject positions available to him the one or ones most appropriate for the particular audience or audiences he was addressing. Sometimes he spoke or wrote primarily as a native of Africa, sometimes as a diasporan African, sometimes as an African Briton, sometimes as a Briton, sometimes as a Christian, and at other times as more than one of the above. Just as we are at the same time parents to our children and children to our parents, our subject position can change while we remain the same. Each of us has overlapping identities, one or more of which dominates in different contexts. Skilled rhetoricians know how to shift their positions, that is, how to emphasize different aspects of their identity to best influence and affect their readers or listeners. The private and public letters, book reviews, and petitions Equiano wrote and published in 1787 and 1788 display a masterful rhetorician honing his skills.

On December 15, 1787, using just the name Gustavus Vassa, Equiano cosigned a letter entitled "The Address of Thanks of the Sons of Africa to the Honourable Granville Sharp, Esq." Only Cugoano and one other cosigner of the letter they sent to the abolitionist Sharp identified themselves with both African and slave names. These self-styled "Sons of Africa" refer to themselves as "we, who are a part, or descendants, of the much-wronged people of Africa" (329, 328).[14] Clearly, Equiano and his colleagues believed that one was as much a "Son of Africa" by descent as by birth. At the end of the eighteenth century, one could be African without ever having set foot in Africa. By the time Equiano published his autobiography, a diasporan African identity was as authentic as a native one.

In writing his autobiography, Equiano transformed a social defect into a rhetorical virtue. Having been dislocated socially and geographically by slavery, he assumed the identity of a "citizen of the world," a cosmopolitan status normally reserved for gentlemen possessing enough wealth and leisure to be able to cultivate tastes that transcended narrow national interests and prejudices (337). Denied a nation, he claimed the world. But if *The Interesting Narrative* is indeed partly historical fiction, what value does it retain for historians?

As a self-proclaimed "citizen of the world," Equiano epitomized what Ira Berlin has called an "Atlantic creole":

> Along the periphery of the Atlantic—first in Africa, then in Europe, and finally in the Americas—[Anglophone-African] society was a product of the momentous meeting of Africans and Europeans and of their equally fateful encounter with the peoples of the Americas. Although the countenances of these new people of the Atlantic—Atlantic creoles—might bear the features of Africa, Europe, or the Americas in whole or in part, their beginnings, strictly speaking, were in none of those places. Instead, by their experiences and sometimes by their persons, they were part of the three worlds that came together along the Atlantic littoral. Familiar with the commerce of the Atlantic, fluent in its new languages, and intimate with its trade and cultures, they were cosmopolitan in the fullest sense.[15]

As an "Atlantic creole," Equiano was ideally positioned to construct an identity for himself. He defined himself as much by movement as by place. Indeed he spent as much of his life on the water as in any place on land. Even while he was a slave, the education and skills he acquired with the Royal Navy rendered him too valuable to be used for the dangerous and backbreaking labor most slaves endured. Service at sea on royal naval and commercial vessels gave him an extraordinary vantage point from which to observe the world around him. His social and geographical mobility exposed him to all kinds of people and levels of Atlantic society. The convincing account of Africa he offered to his readers may have been derived from the experiences of others he tells us he listened to during his many travels in the Caribbean, North America, and Britain. His genius lay in his ability to create and market a voice that for over two centuries has spoken for millions of his fellow diasporan Africans. His value for historians lies in his exemplary status as an "Atlantic creole," whose life and writings demonstrate the challenges and opportunities faced by eighteenth-century citizens of the world.

NOTES

1. W. E. B. Du Bois, "The Negro in Literature and Art," *Annals of the American Academy of Political and Social Science* (September 1913); reprinted in W. E. B. Du Bois, *Writings* (New York: Literary Classics of the United States, 1986), 863.

2. See my "Questioning the Identity of Olaudah Equiano, or Gustavus Vassa, the African," *The Global Eighteenth Century,* ed. Felicity Nussbaum (Baltimore: Johns Hopkins University Press, 2003), 226–35.

3. Adam Hochschild, *Bury the Chains: Prophets and Rebels in the Fight to Free an Empire's Slaves* (Boston: Houghton-Mifflin, 2005), 372.

4. Thomas Clarkson, *An Essay* (London, 1786), 117–18.

5. Quobna Ottobah Cugoano, *Thoughts and Sentiments on the Evil and Wicked Traffic of the Slavery and Commerce of the Human Species,* ed. Vincent Carretta (1787; repr., New York: Penguin, 1999), 15.

6. Kwame Anthony Appiah, *In My Father's House: Africa in the Philosophy of Culture* (New York: Oxford University Press, 1992), 191. I have adapted and applied to Equiano words that Appiah uses to describe the significance of his late father's life: "Only something so particular as a single life—as my father's life, encapsulated in the complex pattern of social and personal relations around his coffin—could capture the multiplicity of our lives in a postcolonial world."

7. Quoted in Appiah, *In My Father's House,* 177.

8. Elizabeth Isichei, *A History of the Igbo People* (New York: St. Martin's Press, 1976), 21. John Thornton, *Africa and Africans in the Making of the Atlantic World, 1400–1800,* 2nd ed. (Cambridge and New York: Cambridge University Press, 1998), 310, notes, "Almost all we know about the [Igbo] region in the eighteenth century comes from the testimony of Olaudah Equiano, an Igbo who was enslaved as a youth around 1755." The fullest treatment of Equiano's claim to an Igbo identity is Alexander Byrd, "Eboe, Country, Nation and Gustavus Vassa's *Interesting Narrative,*" *William and Mary Quarterly* 63 (January 2006): 123–48.

9. The most thorough treatment of the effects the transatlantic slave trade had on the conception and development of African identities during the early modern

period is John Thornton, *Africa and Africans in the Making of the Atlantic World*. On the absence of a pan-Igbo identity in Africa during the eighteenth century, see Sigismund W. Koelle, *Polyglotta Africana* (London, 1854), 7–8; Douglas B. Chambers, "'My Own Nation': Igbo Exiles in the Diaspora," *Slavery and Abolition* 18 (1997): 72–97; Michael Gomez, *Exchanging Our Country Marks: The Transformation of African Identities in the Colonial and Antebellum South* (Chapel Hill: University of North Carolina Press, 1998), 125–26; David Northrup, "Igbo and Myth Igbo: Culture and Ethnicity in the Atlantic World, 1600–1850," *Slavery and Abolition* 21 (2000): 1–20; Chambers, "Ethnicity in the Diaspora: The Slave Trade and the Creation of African 'Nations' in the Americas," *Slavery and Abolition* 22 (2001): 25–39 and "The Significance of the Igbo in the Bight of Biafra Slave-Trade: A Rejoinder to Northrup's 'Myth Igbo,'" *Slavery and Abolition* 23 (2002): 101–20.

10. Elizabeth Isichei, *A History of the Igbo People* (New York: St. Martin's Press, 1976), 21. John Thornton, *Africa and Africans in the Making of the Atlantic World*, 20.

11. Philip D. Morgan, *Slave Counterpoint: Black Culture in the Eighteenth-Century Chesapeake and Lowcountry* (Chapel Hill: University of North Carolina Press, 1998), 62–67. Stephen D. Behrendt, "Markets, Transaction Cycles, and Profits: Merchant Decision Making in the British Slave Trade," *William and Mary Quarterly* 58 (2001): 196.

12. Lorena S. Walsh, "The Chesapeake Slave Trade: Regional Patterns, African Origins, and Some Implications," *William and Mary Quarterly* 58 (2001): 139–70, 153.

13. In "Facts into Fiction: Equiano's *Narrative* Reconsidered," *Research in African Literatures* 13 (1982): 30–43, S. E. Ogude argues that because an eleven-year-old was very unlikely to have the almost total recall Equiano claims, "Equiano relied less on the memory of his experience and more on other sources" (32) in his account of Africa. And in "No Roots Here: On the Igbo Roots of Olaudah Equiano," *Review of English and Literary Studies* 5 (1989): 1–16, Ogude denies that linguistic evidence supports Equiano's account. Despite Ogude's skepticism about Equiano's veracity, he does not question Vassa/Equiano's fundamental identity as an African. G. I. Jones, "Olaudah Equiano of the Niger Ibo," *Africa Remembered: Narratives by West Africans from the Era of the Slave Trade*, ed. Philip D. Curtin (Madison: University of Wisconsin Press, 1967), 60–69, finds Equiano's account of his "home and travels in Nigeria . . . disappointingly brief and confused." He believes that "the little he can remember of his travels is naturally muddled and incoherent" because Equiano "was only eleven years old when he was kidnapped" (61, 69). In her review of Paul Edwards, *The Life of Olaudah Equiano*, and Catherine Obianuju Acholonu, *The Igbo Roots of Olaudah Equiano*, *Journal of African History* 33 (1992): 164–65, Elizabeth Isichei remarks of Equiano's description of Africa, "I have come to believe that it is a palimpsest, and that though he was indeed an Igbo (though even this has been questioned) he fused his own recollections with details obtained from other Igbo into a single version" (165). Katherine Faull Eze, "Self-Encounters: Two Eighteenth-Century African Memoirs from Moravian Bethlehem," in David McBride, LeRoy Hopkins, and C. Aisha Blackshire-Belay, eds., *Crosscurrents: African Americans, Africa,*

and Germany in the Modern World (Columbia, S.C.: Camden House, 1998), 29–52, considers "Equiano's Igbo past [to be] mostly a reconstruction of European or Colonial American travel narratives, most obviously, Anthony Benezet's *Some Historical Account of Guinea,*" 33, 50n22.

14. All quotations from Equiano's works are taken from *The Interesting Narrative and Other Writings,* ed. Vincent Carretta (New York: Penguin, 2003) and are cited by page number parenthetically within the text.

15. Ira Berlin, "From Creole to African: Atlantic Creoles and the Origins of African-American Society in Mainland North America," *William and Mary Quarterly* 33 (1996): 251–88; quotation from 254. I have substituted "Anglophone-African" for Berlin's "African-American" because his characterization of the "Atlantic creole" can be applied to many English-speaking people of African descent on both sides of the Atlantic during the seventeenth and eighteenth centuries. Berlin uses the term *creole* to refer to a person of mixed cultures and languages. During the eighteenth century, a creole was someone of African or European descent who had been born in the Americas.

Construction of Identity

Olaudah Equiano or Gustavus Vassa?

Paul E. Lovejoy

Vincent Carretta claims that recently discovered documents concerning the baptism of Gustavus Vassa and his subsequent employment in the British navy "cast doubt" on the early life of the person usually recognized as Olaudah Equiano, author of *The Interesting Narrative of the Life of Olaudah Equiano, or Gustavus Vassa, the African. Written by Himself.*[1] The two documents in question are his baptismal record at St. Margaret's Church in London and the muster records from the Arctic expedition of Sir John Phipps (later Lord Mulgrave) in 1773, both of which attest to his birth in South Carolina. Carretta casts his web of doubt even broader, suggesting that Vassa/Equiano was born in 1747, not 1745 as claimed in *The Interesting Narrative,* and certainly not in 1742, as I argue in an article appearing in *Slavery and Abolition.*[2] For Carretta, the author of *The Interesting Narrative* was a "self-made" man, adopting a public image as Olaudah Equiano, who had been born in Africa, when in fact he was known as Gustavus Vassa and had been born in South Carolina. For Carretta, "self-made" has a double meaning, including both his success in achieving his emancipation and becoming famous and the fictionalization of his childhood to achieve this end.

Does anyone care where Vassa/Equiano was born? Do a few years difference in when he might have been born matter? I would say the answer to both questions is positive, and Carretta's analysis of the available data is seriously flawed and does not withstand the test of historical methodology. It may seem that the existence of two independent written documents stating place of birth is confirmation that Vassa was born in South Carolina, but if other evidence casts doubt on the documentation, there is a methodological

From *Historically Speaking* 7 (January/February 2006)

challenge that pits memory against documentation. How is cultural information to be interpreted in the light of conflicting documentation, and what is
the context of the documentation that might call the documents themselves
into question or at least blur their possible significance?

According to Carretta, the recent discoveries suggest that "the author of
The Interesting Narrative may have invented rather than reclaimed an African
identity," and if this is the case, then it follows that "he invented his African
childhood and his much-quoted account of the Middle Passage on a slave
ship." In short, documentation for a South Carolina birthplace and problems
in Vassa's own chronology of his youth raise sufficient grounds to express
"reasonable doubt" about Vassa's claim to an African birth. Indeed Carretta
considers that "the burden of proof . . . is now on those who believe that *The
Interesting Narrative* is a historically accurate piece of nonfiction." This
response therefore is in part a reaction to Carretta's challenge that "anyone
who still contends that Equiano's account of the early years of his life is
authentic is obligated to account for the powerful conflicting evidence."

The methodological issues relate to how historians engage oral tradition,
memory, and other nonwritten sources with the written record. The information being conveyed has different meaning if Vassa was born in Africa or in
South Carolina, at least to the historian. If he was an eyewitness to events and
practices in Africa, it is one thing. If it is a composite of stories and information gathered from others, it is another matter, although clearly any account
can be a combination of both. The issue here is whether there is sufficient evidence that Vassa's account of Africa is based on personal observation and
experience or not. Despite some qualifications, Carretta essentially claims
that the first part of *The Interesting Narrative* is a fictionalized account of life
in Africa and the horrors of the Middle Passage, whereas I think that there is
sufficient internal evidence to conclude that the account is essentially authentic, although certainly informed by later reflection, Vassa's acquired knowledge of Africa, and memories of others whom he knew to have come from
the Bight of Biafra. The reflections and memories used in autobiography are
always filtered, but despite this caveat, I would conclude that Vassa was born
in Africa and not in South Carolina.

The significance of this man is not disputed. Vassa was an intellectual and
political figure of heroic proportions. The difference is this: Carretta wants us
to believe that he manufactured an account of his early life because he was
a smart, creative, clever political and intellectual activist. He bent the truth
to achieve a political end, the liberation of his people, and the ending of slavery, first through the abolition of the slave trade and eventually through

emancipation. The political activist and intellectual theorist had to merge the process of enslavement through the violence of kidnapping with the popular mind, gambling aversion to the fear of losing children would put pressure on the few people in Britain who actually voted for Members of Parliament and ultimately Parliament itself. It worked in that Britain abolished the slave trade in 1807, but whether or not Vassa was telling the truth about his birth or making it up for political ends has not been settled, apparently. I certainly agree with Carretta's assessment of Vassa's literary achievements: "He gave a voice to the millions of people forcibly taken from Africa and brought to the Americas as slaves." I think the evidence suggests that his voice was authentic because he personally experienced the Middle Passage. Carretta thinks Vassa was a creative author who used public memory to produce a literary text that was useful in the abolition movement and almost incidentally a work of art. Fraud can produce great art, but so can truth.

The North American connection is also firmly established, whether or not Vassa was born in South Carolina. He was in North America as a slave boy in Virginia, as a slave on a merchant ship and was allowed to trade on his own account, owned by a merchant from Philadelphia, and as an abolitionist in New York and Philadelphia on a visit from London, where he lived. His connection with Philadelphia was important; he must have met abolitionist Anthony Benezet, perhaps through his master, and was impressed by Quakers and their opposition to slavery. Vassa's autobiography had an influence on the slave-narrative literature in North America, probably more so than is yet apparent. How many times his early editions were passed around is simply not known, and there was significant number to require a second North American edition. At least, *The Interesting Narrative* is significant in terms of identification of a literature of resistance and antiracist paradigms advocated by African intellectuals. It can be accepted that Vassa was a man of the "Black Atlantic."

The controversy arises from the interpretation of Vassa's life before the summer of 1754, and here my reconstruction of the early years of Vassa's life varies considerably from that of Carretta. Perhaps we are pursuing historical understanding in different ways, Carretta pushing the evidence that casts doubts on what Vassa says and my own efforts to find out why there are contradictions, assuming that we are dealing with a historic figure who was an honest man and who did NOT deliberately and consciously deceive people. If he had, then he successfully fooled a large number of people in his own day, many of whom were very influential and intelligent. While Carretta appears to have uncovered evidence that Vassa was a fraud and that he knowingly lied,

I am asking the question: what if he was telling the truth? Then how do we account for evidence that conflicts with what he said? Moreover, when would he have invented his narrative, what evidence is there that helps to explain the construction of the narrative, and why would he deliberately have altered his natal home, and if he did, what is the evidence? How old would he have been? How did he sustain the deception, if he constructed an African birth but in fact was born in South Carolina? What are his reflections on being in South Carolina later in his life? The fact that he worked for Dr. Charles Irving on the Arctic expedition in 1773 and later was involved with Irving in the abortive plantation scheme on the Mosquito Shore in 1776 has not been examined carefully. On the Arctic expedition, Vassa registered his birth as being in South Carolina, while Irving hired him for the Mosquito Shore venture because he could speak the language of his "countrymen," that is, Igbo. The seemingly irrefutable evidence of the two documents is brought into question when examined in context.

The biggest lacuna in Carretta's scholarship is the answer to this question: where did Vassa learn his understanding of Igbo cosmology and society, indeed his knowledge of the Igbo language, as revealed in the vocabulary that he mentions in *The Interesting Narrative?* Did he learn it in the Carolinas before he was sold to Pascal? This is unlikely, since there were few Igbo in South Carolina, and he was not in Virginia long enough to meet anyone with whom he could speak, according to his own testimony, even though there were relatively many Igbo in the tidewater region. He was only there seven weeks, by his own account, which no one has disputed, and he met no one with whom he could speak. He clearly did not speak English, although by this time if he had come from Africa, he would have probably have begun to learn some words. If he had been born in South Carolina, he would have known English in the form spoken on plantations, a pidgin but nonetheless English. If he did understand Igbo, then, where and when did he learn it? A birth in Igboland and close contact with people who spoke his language of birth, that is, other speakers of the Igbo language, until he was almost twelve answers these questions. Does a birth in South Carolina suggest as conclusive evidence of origins? I would suggest not.

According to Carretta, Vassa's "account of Africa is a combination of printed sources, memory, and imagination," presumably Carretta means the memory of others who were responsible for what he was told, since Carretta believes him to have been born in South Carolina. This conception of memory seems to merge into "imagination," and hence fiction, but is it really safe to conclude that because Vassa had great literary skills that he made it up? I think not, although he understood how to use language to convey a poignant story that in its telling might influence history, which it did. Anthony Benezet has been cited as a source, and it is clear that Benezet was an influence on Vassa's political development, which he duly acknowledges in *The Interesting Narrative*. But what could Vassa have learned? A close reading of Benezet's books and pamphlets reveals that he had absolutely nothing to say about Igboland or Igbo culture and society.[3] His work, with its noble polemics of antislavery, is nothing more than long quotes, within quotation marks, of different sources to prove Benezet's point that slavery was evil and that everything possible should be done to stamp it out and abolish the slave trade. Benezet's ideological and moral position was an important influence in Vassa's comprehension of the political and religious aspects of abolition, but he was not a source of information on Africa. Vassa's reference to Benin, Libya, and Abyssinia are all clearly intended to situate his own people within the "Africa" with which he had come to identify.

Who were Vassa's confidants when he was writing *The Interesting Narrative* in 1788? And what did they believe? Why would they buy into a fraud, and what evidence is there for anyone doing so? Vassa was a person of principle, and he was an astute political observer. Rather than commit a fraud to achieve a political end of humanitarian proportions, he actually told the truth, at least there is overwhelming evidence that suggests as much. Carretta asks the question: "Why might Equiano have created an African nativity and disguised an American birth?" I would ask, When would he have done this, and what textual evidence is there for the invention, despite the baptismal register and the Arctic muster role? The evidence suggests that he knew Igbo as a language and had had personal contact with Igbo culture as a child. If he had manufactured this information, when could he have done it and on the basis of what authority?

According to Carretta, "Despite claiming to describe distinctively Igbo manners, he [Vassa] conflates accounts of various African ethnic groups to construct a kind of pan-African identity, a sort of essential African." Carretta does not make it clear which ethnic groups are conflated, and I would argue, to the contrary, Vassa provides the earliest information on several important Igbo institutions, including some insight into how these institutions operated before the middle of the eighteenth century. Most important, in my opinion, is Vassa's description of the *ichi* facial markings and their significance. Carretta's conclusion on the process of how ethnicity played itself out in the interior of the Bight of Biafra is based on no authority, while Vassa's account is compatible with the findings of numerous historians who have studied the interior of the Bight of Biafra. Indeed I would assert that Vassa's description of his country and his people is sufficient confirmation that he was born where he said he was and, based on when boys received the *ichi* scarification, that he was about eleven when he was kidnapped, as he claims, which suggests a birth date of ca. 1742, not 1745 or 1747. A shift in the chronology this way is warranted on the basis of internal evidence in *The Interesting Narrative* and the fact that Pascal arrived in England in December 1754 with the slave boy he had named Gustavus Vassa.

If Carretta is correct about Vassa's age at time of baptism, accepting the documentary evidence, then he was a boy too young to have created a complex fraud about origins. If he were as old as I think he was at the time of baptism, he might have been able to have constructed such a story, but there is little proof that he did and some proof that he did not. The fraud must have been perpetrated later, but when? Certainly the baptismal record cannot be used as proof that he committed fraud, only that his godparents might have. But why would they have done so is the question, not what a slave might have said in St. Margaret's Church, where the Members of Parliament met for morning prayers before opening session. Vassa was in the sanctuary of power, probably the only slave ever baptized in St. Margaret's, and he was given a birthplace of South Carolina. Was this a social event, a fraud of another kind, a joke? He was, after all, none other than Gustavus Vassa, the savior of his people, named after the liberator of Sweden, and seems to have believed that he had been promised manumission on baptism. The text itself points to authenticity, not fraud. It is the detail in the baptismal registry that requires explanation. As Carretta observes, Vassa provides details during and after the Seven Years' War, which, when possible to verify, are remarkably accurate.

Vassa's description of Igbo cultural features are not generic African practices or some garbled merging of accounts, as has been claimed. Moreover, Carretta is not accurate in stating that "Modern scholars rightly point out that of the surviving brief eighteenth-century descriptions of the kingdom of Benin, Equiano's account of Igboland is the most fully developed." In my opinion, this is inaccurate because Vassa's account has nothing to do with the Kingdom of Benin, which Vassa added to his narrative on the basis of reading Benezet, who specifically did not discuss Igboland. Vassa was attempting to situate what he knew within the framework of what was known about Africa, and similarly he used such terms as *Libyan* and *Ethiopian* to try to achieve the same results. He also contrasted his people with Jews and Muslims, once again to establish similarities and differences with his own memories of his homeland. The relationship with the Kingdom of Benin is in fact plausible, but only parts of Igboland west of the Niger River were tributary to Benin in the eighteenth century, and the area that Vassa was from almost certainly was not that part of Igboland but rather central Igboland to the east of the Niger River. While Vassa drew on published sources for what he knew about other parts of Africa, there is nothing in any of the known sources that he used that actually has anything to say about Igboland. His information has to have been derived from his own experience, whatever he learned in London from some of his own "countrymen."

According to Carretta, "critics and scholars have increasingly come to recognize that his account's apparent uniqueness does not guarantee its authenticity." In support of this contention, Carretta refers to various critics, including S. E. Ogude, who have seemed to have criticized the "Igboness" of Vassa's account, although it seems to me that the concerns of these critics are with issues of orthography and Vassa's attempts to render complex concepts understandable to an audience that had no knowledge of Africa and in which he himself had only partially understood as a boy. Ogude's criticisms are intended to demonstrate the difficulty of establishing where a boy named Equiano might have come from in Igboland, not that he did not come from there. Despite the identification of key Igbo words and concepts, it is not possible to be certain about the dialect, and hence Vassa's identification with a particular part of Igboland remains in doubt.

Vassa was one of the first to say he was an African and, in accordance with contemporary usage in Europe, to be equated with Ethiopians and Libyans. As Alexander Byrd has demonstrated, Vassa's use of these concepts reflects evolving meanings of nation and citizenship as discussed in the late eighteenth century.[4] The term *Eboe* as used by Vassa had various meanings. In the eighteenth century, apparently, it was not a term that described a common ethnic identity because its implication was pejorative; it meant "other" people, both neighbors and foreigners, but who presumably spoke a dialect of Igbo and who in fact would now be recognized as Igbo. Vassa's use of these various terms and others, such as "countrymen" and "nation," are important examples of how Vassa and, by extension, others from Africa and of African descent were grappling with issues of identity and community.

Hence, it may appear that Carretta has a good case, much better than that of Vassa's critics who first challenged his claim of an African birth in 1792. The baptism record states age and place of birth, as does the Arctic muster book, despite differences in the derived date of birth, the baptism record suggesting a date of birth in 1747 and the Arctic list indicating 1745. The weakness in Carretta's argument arises from his understanding of the ethnography and history of the interior of the Bight of Biafra. Moreover, Carretta's chronology for Vassa's life is not supported by the available evidence, and it is more likely that Vassa was born before he says he was, rather than later. This reconstruction suggests that he was about twelve when he first arrived in England, as he states in *The Interesting Narrative,* which we know to have been in December 1754. If he had been born in 1747, as Carretta has concluded, it is unlikely that he could have earned his freedom between 1763 and 1766, in fact earning much more than the cost of his ransom because he suffered from theft and nonpayment, which would have meant that be earned his freedom by the time he was nineteen. If this was the case, he would have been a most unusual young man indeed. If, however, he was born in 1742, he would have been baptized when he was seventeen, earning his freedom by the time he was twenty-four, which seems more plausible.

NOTES

1. Olaudah Equiano, *The Interesting Narrative and Other Writings,* ed. Vincent Carretta (New York: Penguin, 2003).

2. Paul E. Lovejoy, "Autobiography and Memory: Gustavus Vassa, alias Olaudah Equiano, the African," *Slavery and Abolition* 27 (2006): 317–47.

3. Anthony Benezet, *Some Historical Account of Guinea, Its Situation, Produce and the General Disposition of its Inhabitants with an Inquiry into the Rise and Progress of the Slave Trade, Its Nature and Lamentable Effects* (1771; London: Frank Cass, 1968). Benezet quoted at length various European observations of western Africa but nothing on the interior of the Bight of Biafra, skipping from the Kingdom of Benin to Kongo and Angola in his descriptions and reports. He quotes some information on Barbados that presumably Vassa could have used but not on his homeland.

4. Alexander X. Byrd, "Eboe, Country, Nation and Gustavus Vassa's *Interesting Narrative,*" *William and Mary Quarterly* 63 (January 2006): 123–48.

Good-bye, Equiano, the African

Trevor Burnard

O ne of the interesting narratives in political and intellectual life in the last decade has been the reappearance of old-fashioned concerns about the importance of being truthful and the irretrievable damage that being caught in a lie does to a person's character. Whatever Bill Clinton did as president is overshadowed by his lie about his encounters with an intern that led him to falsely claim that "I did not have sex with that woman." Tony Blair's distinguished record is diminished for many Britons who, like me, believed him when he said that Iraq had weapons of mass destruction. In intellectual life, proponents of postmodernism suffered grievous blows when the postmodernist literary theorist Paul de Man was exposed as having obscured portions of his earlier life and suffered again when Alan Sokal, a physicist, submitted successfully a deliberately ridiculous article to a leading postmodernist journal. Periodic controversies about people assuming identities that were fabricated keep on emerging, such as when the distinguished scholar of early America Joseph Ellis was alleged to have invented a story about himself as a Vietnam War veteran. What is significant in all these cases is that the lie mattered, even in the last instance, where the lie was not related to what Ellis did. No one has suggested that Ellis writes untruths in his published work. Yet his rather harmless fabrication of a war past led to public humiliation.

Questions about lying have also become increasingly important in understanding the past, dramatically so in early American history, especially in the history of slavery. The biggest controversy has surrounded Thomas Jefferson, who has been shown, pretty much conclusively, to have fathered children with his slave Sally Hemings.[1] Less well publicized but of as much moment has been Michael Johnson's devastating demolition of a century-long scholarship that presumed that Denmark Vesey was the leader of a putative slave

From *Historically Speaking* 7 (January/February 2006)

revolt in Charleston in 1822.[2] Another controversy has surrounded the discovery by Henry Louis Gates Jr. of a novel, *The Bondswoman's Narrative*, by Hannah Crafts, which Gates claimed as the only surviving novel about slavery written by an American female ex-slave. The problem here is that conclusive proof that the author was an ex-slave is missing. Although it probably shouldn't matter when evaluating literary excellence, whether Crafts was black or not makes all the difference in the world. As Gates notes in the case of Emma Dunham Kelly-Hawkins, a writer once thought to be black and now known to be white, when black writers are redefined as white, "people won't write about her any more," because what is important is discovering black voices not interesting new white writers.[3]

To my mind, the most intriguing discovery that a fundamental text in African American writing is not what it seems has been made by Vincent Carretta about Olaudah Equiano's *Interesting Narrative*. Carretta has discovered evidence—not conclusive but compelling enough for him to consider it more likely to be true than to be false—that Equiano was not an African but was probably born as a slave in South Carolina, of Igbo descent. Thus his vivid recollections of his childhood in Africa, his enslavement and transportation to the coast, and the trauma of the Middle Passage are inventions, "combinations of printed sources, memory, and imagination." Equiano was unable to resist, Carretta implies, the siren lure of becoming an authentic African voice describing the horrors of the transatlantic slave trade at a time when the abolitionist movement most needed such a voice. In market terms (and Equiano was acutely attuned to marketplace concerns—his construction of an Igbo identity was not a disinterested intellectual act but brought him sizeable financial benefits), Equiano saw a market need for a first-hand account of how Africans experienced the Middle Passage and proceeded to supply that voice, creating in the process an Igbo identity that probably did not exist at the time. If we accept Carretta's contention that Equiano was actually an American slave who had never lived in Africa, then Equiano is guilty of perpetrating two lies. He pretended to be offering an authentic account of himself as a victim of one of the great crimes in Western history when he was not a victim—partly in order to advance an honorable cause, partly to make money. He also invented himself as an Igbo and attempted to create, through his writings, a pan-Igbo identity that suggests more connections between peoples in Africa than actually existed. These are serious charges, which should lead us, in my opinion, to question whether Vassa is a reliable witness in other areas and which, by casting doubt upon his truthfulness, should also lead us to be more suspicious of his character and less effusive about his "genius," as Carretta sees it, and his "exemplary status as an 'Atlantic creole.'"

The new findings about Olaudah Equiano, or Gustavus Vassa, are the most difficult to deal with of all the recent reevaluations of what seemed to be established historical fact in the history of slavery in the Americas. We can cope with the fact that Jefferson had a private secret that made his relationship with black slavery particularly complicated. Scandals that discredit revered dead white men suit the mores of our cynical age. Finding out that the Denmark Vesey conspiracy existed only in the imaginings of South Carolinian slaveholders allows us to recast our attention with profit away from dealing with actual slave conspiracies toward an examination, along the lines we do with outbreaks of witchcraft hysteria in Salem, of why black behavior could encourage whites into panics about illusory slave plots.[4] We can also accept that Hannah Crafts was not an ex-slave or even a black woman because in dealing with a novel, we do not mind as much as in other works whether the work is "true" or whether the author is as she says she is, provided that the work itself has, as several critics have claimed, an underlying power and aesthetic importance.[5]

But discovering that Equiano was probably not an African and that he probably made up his arresting passages on how he was enslaved as a child and transported across on the Middle Passage is a different matter, primarily because the authenticity of his account is so crucial to its lasting significance. We don't read *The Interesting Narrative* because it is well written, although Equiano does write well. We don't read it, moreover, in the way that Carretta seems to suggest it might now be read, as an intriguing example of how an African American could become a self-made man by refashioning his identity in response to changing circumstances. We read *The Interesting Narrative* because it is *true;* because it is an eyewitness account—the only one we have from a direct participant in the slave trade—of the cruelties of the Middle Passage, in particular, and Atlantic slavery, in general. The passages from *The Interesting Narrative* that are most used by teachers are precisely those whose authenticity is now most suspect. Equiano has become a canonical text because it has the ring of authenticity. We assign Equiano as a text because, as one teacher puts it, students "enjoy reading the first-person account of a well-educated and resourceful former slave whose life story is filled with remarkable adventures and great achievements."[6] If it is not a first-person account of the travails of an African, then its appeal diminishes considerably. Indeed its appeal declines so much so that we can no longer use Equiano as a guide to the Middle Passage, painful as jettisoning his vivid prose about this crucial event is to our strategies for making it understandable.

Moreover, once we doubt whether Equiano was an African, it becomes harder, contra Carretta, to believe him in other areas. I have, for example, always had my doubts about the provenance of his name: I have surveyed thousands of slave names in Jamaica and have never come across a name as outlandish as Gustavus Vassa. It also becomes more difficult to treat him, as Carretta urges us to do, as someone who can be relied upon to speak for others. Why would we allow a fabulist to do this? I can see Carretta's problem— his project was intended to praise Equiano, not to diminish him, and he has written a biography about the man—but I think that as well as reassessing how we interpret and use his autobiography, we need to reassess the man himself. Carretta always gives Equiano the benefit of the doubt. He is a "skillful and careful" writer. He gave a "voice" to millions of Africans, despite not perhaps being African himself, begging an obvious question of who should be allowed to speak for whom. He was a "pioneer" in creating an Igbo national identity—an identity that increasingly seems like a fabrication. He is "an even more profoundly self-made man than Franklin," implicitly making a virtue out of his mistruths by equating him with another canonical figure in early American literature. He is a "masterful rhetorician," whose shifting identities, some real, some invented, can be seen as not only natural but also admirably effective. In fact, Carretta concludes, it doesn't matter whether Equiano was an African or just pretended to be one, because "a diasporan African identity was as authentic as a native one."

I beg to differ. If indeed Equiano was American, not African (and it should be noted that Carretta's doubts about his identity are founded on strong circumstantial evidence rather than on hard fact), then he has lied about the most important feature of his life. His detractors at the time recognized that it was his status as an authentic African voice that gave his account its power. The *Oracle* newspaper raised doubts about Equiano's parentage in 1792, claiming he was born in the West Indies. Significantly it concluded that the abolitionist cause would be damaged if it leant "for support on falsehoods as audaciously propagated as they are easily detected." Equiano recognized the danger and castigated the newspaper for "invidious falsehoods" designed to "hurt my character, and to discredit and prevent the sale of my Narrative."[7] He was aware that a customary charge made against slaves and Africans were that they were habitual liars, able to mimic the works of others but unable to create anything fresh unaided by white assistance. Not being a liar was thus doubly important. It confirmed his victim status as genuine and proved that Africans were as capable as whites of writing believable and *true* narratives. If, however, Equiano was actually a liar, not a truth teller, then not only was a voice from Africa lost but also what racists said about Africans and their tendency to lie was correct. I don't think those writers were correct in their estimation of the African character, but Equiano's elaborations, even though made in a good cause, make such a contention less plausible than it should be. For this reason, although we would love to have a first-hand account such as that in *The Interesting Narrative* that brings alive the Middle Passage and New World slavery, we have to say good-bye to Equiano as a guide to that experience. He may remain important as an example of black self-fashioning but in the great scheme of things, such importance is of limited and specialized interest. We may have to accept that, as Primo Levi argued for understanding the Holocaust, "the survivors are not the true witnesses" because the "true witnesses" are the "drowned, the submerged, the annihilated."[8] In my opinion, Equiano cannot remain a central figure in the reconstruction of the Atlantic world unless the doubt that Carretta has cast upon his authenticity as an African disappears.

NOTES

1. "Forum: Thomas Jefferson and Sally Hemings Redux," *William and Mary Quarterly*, 3rd ser., 57 (2000): 121–210.

2. Michael Johnson, "Denmark Vesey and His Co-Conspirators," *William and Mary Quarterly*, 3rd ser., 58 (2001): 915–76.

3. Elaine Showalter and English Showalter, "Every Single One Matters," *London Review of Books*, August 18, 2005.

4. "The Making of a Slave Conspiracy, part 2," *William and Mary Quarterly*, 3d Ser., 59 (2002): 166, 177–78.

5. Nina Baym, "The Case for Hannah Vincent," in *In Search of Hannah Crafts: Critical Essays on "The Bondwoman's Narrative,"* ed. Henry Louis Gates Jr. and Hollis Robbins (Basic Books, 2004), 315–31.

6. Angelo Costanzo, "Olaudah Equiano (1745–1797)," Houghton Mifflin College Division, http://college.hmco.com/English/heath/syllabuild/iguide/vassa.html (accessed February 18, 2008).

7. Quoted in Vincent Carretta, "Questioning the Identity of Olaudah Equiano, or Gustavus Vassa, the African," in *The Global Eighteenth Century*, ed. Felicity A. Nussbaum (Baltimore: Johns Hopkins University Press, 2003), 227–28.

8. Primo Levi, *The Drowned and the Saved* (New York: Summit, 1988), ix.

Beyond Equiano

Jon Sensbach

O f course Olaudah Equiano matters. Vincent Carretta contends that the eighteenth-century's best-known person of African descent might have been born in South Carolina rather than in West Africa, as Equiano claimed in his autobiography. Whether we agree or not with Carretta—and I find his evidence quite intriguing—we'll read Equiano differently now and perhaps even more urgently. The possibility that he was born in America makes him more interesting, not less so; it opens up, rather than forecloses, inquiry into the autobiography and the world in which its author moved, giving new vitality to a man who's become something of a stick figure in recent years. For all the layers of meaning in his life's narrative, we'll need to excavate many more now. Whatever his birthplace, his autobiography remains the gold standard for the genre. So, yes, Equiano still matters. At the same time, this new version of his life poses new questions about the eighteenth-century black Atlantic that transcend its enigmatic exemplar himself.

It's easy to see how Equiano, after being virtually forgotten for 150 years, became an icon again in the late twentieth century. For modern students eager to hear the voice of the people, his story bears the same authentic witness to the slave trade and African survival as it did for antislavery activists two centuries ago. In our own writing and teaching, he's an irresistible resource, always handy with a quote or anecdote from his amazing "I was there" exploits to make the point for us. What were conditions like during the Middle Passage? Equiano endured them; through his description, we imagine the stench and shudder. How did African captives from different language groups communicate? He overheard their conversations through middlemen and learned several new languages himself; he'll tell us. What was it like for a young Igbo boy in America to hear a book "talk" for the first time?

From *Historically Speaking* 7 (January/February 2006)

Undergraduates don't have to take the professor's word for it—they can read that memorable passage for themselves.

Equiano's autobiography, as Nell Painter has remarked, "works as a kind of founding myth for African American history," an epic tale of idyllic African life, Atlantic slavery, American self-liberation, and international leadership for human rights—one man's narrative of progress and redemption that represents the struggles of millions.[1] Equiano can be whatever we want him to be, equally popular among historians and literary scholars alike and a convenient bridge between them. When "identity" and "self-fashioning" became the buzzwords of the 1990s for both groups, Equiano furnished the perfect memoir to show how those slippery concepts could be applied to African narrators during the age of the slave trade.

Above all, as Carretta rightly notes, Equiano is a classic Atlantic creole, that new breed of people shaped not only by the confluence of Africa, Europe, and the Americas but by their own movement across and around the ocean between those points, a hybrid transnational group adept at maneuvering among a medley of people, languages, and situations. Creoles embodied a defining irony of the world that produced them. Scholars generally define the "Atlantic world" of the early modern period as the integrated and cohesive product of economic, social, and intellectual capital that flowed in many directions across the ocean—"a unitary whole, a single system," as Philip Morgan has described it.[2] Yet the lives of Atlantic creoles were anything but unified. Deploying multiple identities was their way of negotiating chaos and uncertainty, not coherence. We usually hail that strategy as a positive survival mechanism to cope with a system heavily weighted against them. But while we can applaud the creoles' savvy adaptability, we can forget that they were casualties of the Atlantic system as well, uprooted outcasts grasping for meaning and stability in a world that offered little.

In the light of Carretta's new version of Equiano's life, then, the question becomes: what kind of Atlantic creole was he? The answer is crucial. In his own time and in ours, an African birth validates his eyewitness claims to authenticity when describing his Igbo upbringing, his capture and tortuous forced journey to the African coast, and the Middle Passage, even though Equiano apparently drew upon other writers for these descriptions as well. In this scenario, originating directly from the African wellspring, he accumulates many layers of Atlantic acculturation as his life unfolds, eventually staking a claim to a black British identity. If, on the other hand, he had never been to Africa and never witnessed the Middle Passage, he becomes a very different and, in some ways, more complex creole whose memoir now calls for different readings that account for the vividness and rhetorical impact of his descriptions.

Imagine, for example, that as a young boy in mid-eighteenth-century South Carolina, Equiano grows up surrounded by speakers of Gullah, Igbo, and other African languages in a community where memories of Africa and the slave trade are alive and raw. Perhaps he absorbs and remembers as many stories as he can, acting as a kind of oral historian, a funnel or repository for communal memory. Later in life, as he gains literacy, facility in English, freedom, and mobility, he finds the opportunity—and feels an obligation—to use these stories in the antislavery struggle. He supplements these, as Carretta notes, with tales told him by many others during the course of his travels, repackaging them as his own to add veracity he knows white activists crave.

In this scenario—unprovable, yet no more fanciful than any other one can imagine in the face of conflicting evidence—a South Carolinian birth does not necessarily invalidate Equiano's story but recasts it with a different kind of authenticity. If he did not endure the Middle Passage himself, how else would he have learned about it and reported on it so persuasively from the perspective of the captives themselves but by listening, at some point, somewhere, to those who had? Proslavery defenders always contended that narratives of former slaves like Equiano were ghostwritten by white abolitionists, but perhaps it is closer to the truth that Equiano is a kind of ghostwriter for dozens or hundreds of people whose experiences live on in his words. He becomes a witness in the larger sense, testifying on behalf of people who had seen what he had not. Whatever is not strictly "true" in the narrative—whatever he did not actually see or do what he said he did—becomes a kind of larger Truth in its universalism. In that regard, the importance of his birthplace recedes in the face of his visionary politics. Equiano transforms himself from Carolina creole into "citizen of the world," spokesman for all people of African descent caught or at peril of being caught in the dragnet of slavery—a diasporan "Son of Africa," as Carretta suggests, and perhaps its first Afro-Atlantic griot with a chance to record his story.

Debates about Equiano's origins will furnish new ways of analyzing his autobiography for a long time; indeed, all of his observations now can potentially be reinterpreted as those of an American-born writer rather than of an African. Scholars of precolonial Africa, especially of Igbo culture and of the workings of the slave trade in West Africa and at sea, might need to reevaluate long-held assumptions. At the same time, even as we pause to reassess Equiano, we can profitably look for ways to use the lessons of his narrative to move beyond him. If Equiano's chief importance is as an exemplary Atlantic creole, then his story should encourage us to broaden the search for other compelling figures from the age of the slave trade who can tell us things he cannot. Because of the long shadow cast by his narrative, Equiano has become an archetype, perhaps even a stereotype, of the black Atlantic—Anglophone, ex-slave, Christian, memoirist, often a sailor, invariably male. All of the most frequently anthologized ex-slave narrators from the eighteenth century—Venture Smith, James Albert Gronniosaw, John Marrant, John Jea, David George, and Equiano himself—meet nearly all of these criteria. Of course we like our source material to be accessible, and it is natural enough that we privilege authors over those who left no written record of their lives. As such, Equiano and, to a lesser extent, that small handful of other figures have become stand-ins for the vast numbers of unnamed people who could not speak or write for themselves and whose travails went unremembered. But it sometimes seems that we have allowed our reliance on these autobiographies to shape and limit the questions we ask and to keep us from digging deeper and wider for sources into other kinds of Atlantic experience.

As Equiano demonstrates, we can learn much from a single life played out in diverse corners of the Atlantic littoral, a life characterized by movement, by pliable identities, by intermingling with and sliding between a kaleidoscope of people and languages, and by a determination to find order amid chaos. It's remarkable that we still know of so few such lives, but I'm convinced there are more of them out there than we suspect, people we haven't looked for or haven't realized can be found, people who moved around more commonly than we think between American destinations, Europe, and even Africa itself, and whose stories can be told in greater detail than we imagine. We won't necessarily find them in the usual places. They will come from far more heterogeneous points on the Atlantic compass—from Portuguese, French, Spanish, Dutch, German, or even unknown English documents, lying in overlooked boxes in an archive in Paris, Lisbon, Havana, Amsterdam, or Accra, perhaps in an unexpected provincial archive somewhere. Their biographies, when and wherever we can find them, might not be as well documented as Equiano's, and they may lack the firsthand power of his narrative. But they will be extensive enough to remind us, as his does, of the humanity of the millions snared in the slave trade and of the incredible diversity of their identities—Angolan, Koromantee, Brazilian, Jamaican, French, Muslim, Catholic, Lutheran, escapee, soldier, preacher, victim, survivor, male, female. A central figure in my own research, Rebecca Protten, was a free person of color in the eighteenth century who spoke Dutch, Danish, German, and English, helped organize black Christian congregations in the Caribbean, lived in Germany for twenty years, and spent the last years of her life on the Gold Coast. Such lives and those of others we might reconstruct reaffirm that there was no quintessential Atlantic creole personality or experience but that the multiplicity of experiences is itself the defining feature of the black Atlantic.

Equiano never claimed to be the quintessence of anything, but he did claim to be representative. More than two hundred years later, he still is, though what he represented in his time and what he represents in our own have, thanks largely to Carretta, become more complicated questions. Yes, Equiano matters.

NOTES

1. Nell Painter, quoted in Jennifer Howard, "Unraveling the Narrative," *Chronicle of Higher Education*, September 9, 2005, 3.

2. Philip D. Morgan, "The Cultural Implications of the Atlantic Slave Trade: African Regional Origins, American Destinations, and New World Developments," *Slavery and Abolition* 18 (1997): 122.

Response to Lovejoy, Burnard, and Sensbach

Vincent Carretta

T he three responses elicited by my initial essay fall into two distinct categories. Burnard and Sensbach, coming to opposite conclusions, consider possible implications of the recently discovered evidence in baptismal and naval records that suggest that Equiano may have invented an African birth. Lovejoy, however, challenges the validity of the evidence by mocking the sincerity of the baptismal record and ignoring the questions raised by the muster lists in 1773. Since Lovejoy also says that my "analysis of the available data is seriously flawed and does not withstand the test of historical methodology," I feel a bit like Equiano, who believed that some of his critics wrote "with a view to hurt [his] character, and to discredit and prevent the sale of [his] book." And like Equiano, I feel compelled to issue an apologia in my own defense.

I am grateful to Lovejoy for citing my recently published biography, *Equiano, the African: Biography of a Self-Made Man* (2005). Lovejoy acknowledges that "perhaps we are pursuing historical understanding in different ways." I agree completely and would add that we argue "in different ways" as well. Assuming that the historian's role is to reconstruct and interpret the past in the light of the available evidence and that speculation (like faith) should begin when the evidence runs out, as an editor, biographer, and historian I began with the working hypothesis that Equiano was being as truthful as possible in writing his autobiography. I also assume that my hypothesis must be falsifiable, subject to possible revision or rejection in the face of new evidence. And I assume that conclusions drawn from the evidence, as well as speculation beyond the evidence, should be located on a spectrum ranging from the impossible through the improbable and probable to the certain. I am obligated to give my readers the evidence they need to appreciate my assessment of it and to be able to assess it for themselves. Consequently, constrained by my methodology, I cannot say, as Lovejoy does, that Equiano "must have met abolitionist Anthony Benezet" in Philadelphia, without offering some evidence in support.

If we can identify the tree by the fruit it bears, Lovejoy's methodology is more supple and liberating than my own. So, too, is his understanding of argument. He appears to subscribe to a school of literary critics who believe that a writer's intentions cannot be derived from his or her writings. Consequently the critic bears the responsibility for determining meaning in a text, which may be "read against the grain," allowing the critic to divine that the writer means something different from, even opposite to, what he or she actually says. Lovejoy exercises his powers of divination on my own writings. Thus, although he initially accurately quotes me as saying that "the author of *The Interesting Narrative* may have invented rather than reclaimed an African identity," a paragraph later we learn that "despite some qualifications, Carretta essentially claims that the first part of *The Interesting Narrative* is a fictionalized account." The argumentative slope rapidly becomes slipperier. Several lines later we learn that "Carretta wants us to believe that he manufactured an account of his early life." And within a few more paragraphs we are in free fall: "Carretta believes him to have been born in South Carolina," and we discover that "Carretta has concluded" that "he had been born in 1747." Understandably, once we get on the slippery slope of this line of reasoning, the quotations from my writings disappear.

Although I confess that I find it interesting to be told what I mean, I might have been more convinced had Lovejoy devoted more space to quoting what I actually say. Readers of this forum can judge for themselves the extent to which I qualify my analysis of the likelihood that Equiano may have fabricated an African birth to achieve the dual and complementary ends of serving the abolitionist cause and making money. Look at the number of times the words *may, might, if,* and *whether* appear in my initial essay and other writings on the subject. If I have foreclosed the possibility that Equiano's account of an African birth and upbringing is accurate, why have I spent so much energy trying to identify the ships that may have brought Equiano from Africa to Barbados and from there to Virginia? I thought I did so because, as I have said repeatedly, the circumstantial evidence that Equiano was born in South Carolina may be persuasive, but it is not conclusive, dispositive though not probative. Lovejoy seems to confuse inclination with conviction. I assume that when I disagree with someone I am obligated to represent that person's position as accurately as possible.

Lovejoy's own convictions lead to some intriguing argumentation. Evidence can falsify my hypothesis; Lovejoy's thesis that Equiano was born in Africa apparently can falsify evidence. I do not have space here to treat the minute particulars of his discoveries, such as a hitherto unknown "second North American edition" of Equiano's autobiography. Lovejoy slides effortlessly from supposition to certainty. He begs the question he raises of whether Equiano was fluent in Igbo by asserting that "Irving hired him for the Mosquito Shore venture because he could speak the language of his 'countrymen,' that is, Igbo," without offering any evidence to support his claim for Irving's motive. Nor does he consider qualification and annotation Equiano added to "countrymen" in later editions, additions very problematic for his assertion. Irving is mentioned in a non sequitur to the briefest of allusions to what for Lovejoy is probably a very annoying piece of evidence, the 1773 muster lists for the Arctic expedition on which Equiano, now a free man and the source of the information, is identified three separate times as having been born in South Carolina. Lovejoy does not even apply his powers of divination to attempt to explain why Equiano would have said he was born in America just fifteen years before he would claim in print an African birth. Lovejoy might have suggested that Equiano was trying to keep the naval record consistent with his earlier baptismal record, but he forecloses that opportunity by mockingly dismissing the latter with the question, "Was this a social event, a fraud of another kind, a joke?" To do so, Lovejoy must completely ignore Equiano's own comments about the piety of his godparents, his desire to be baptized, and Pascal's resistance. Apparently sometimes Equiano is reliable and sometimes not. As literary critic, Lovejoy gets to choose.

One choice Lovejoy makes is to reject both Equiano's own claim to a birth date of 1745 and his baptismal record's date of circa 1747. As I have said several times in print, both dates can at best be only approximate, and *if* either is correct, Equiano was younger than he says he was when he entered an English-speaking environment. Very few biological markers indicate age before adulthood: one is the loss of baby teeth around the age of seven; another is the onset of puberty. Explicitly accepting my discovery that Equiano first reached England in December 1754, years before he claims, and implicitly embracing my argument that the younger Equiano was when he came under Pascal's control the less credible his account of Africa would have been, Lovejoy has little choice but to imagine a date of birth significantly earlier than 1747. His supposition, however, has unanticipated consequences. Employing logic that I confess eludes me, Lovejoy argues that since Equiano had not "received the *ichi* scarification," he "was about eleven when he was kidnapped." Even if we accept Lovejoy's assumption that Equiano was taken from Africa, where he would have been destined to receive the scarification after the onset of puberty, all that the absence of such marking would prove was that he was younger than eleven but not necessarily eleven. Boys in the Royal Navy ranged in age from six to eighteen. Pascal's promotion of Equiano in late 1762, when he was around the age of eighteen according to Equiano's own and the documentary evidence, thus makes sense. Lovejoy would have him in his early twenties at the time. For the 1759 baptismal record, which says that Equiano was twelve years old, to be off by a year or two before puberty is plausible. But to have it off by five years, as Lovejoy contends, should place Equiano well into puberty at the age of seventeen. As a seventeen-year-old, he would have been far more likely to have had a say in what was recorded and to have later remembered what was recorded. And his godparents and witnesses should have noticed the difference between a child and an adolescent. Lovejoy completely avoids the question of why in his autobiography Equiano suppresses the records of a South Carolina birth. My methodology requires me to at least attempt to account for why those records exist in fact and why they are absent in his narration. But, as Lovejoy supposes, "we are pursuing historical understanding in different ways."

Lovejoy's questions about why Equiano might have fabricated an identity and why such a fabrication would not have been discovered or betrayed are sufficiently answered, I hope, in my initial essay and other writings, especially the biography. In the latter I trace as carefully as I can the evolution of Equiano's African identity before he published his *Interesting Narrative.* Whether or not he fabricated that identity, Equiano very likely knew that the problematic baptismal and naval records existed. He might have acknowledged them in his *Narrative* and explained their existence. Instead, assuming that he had not forgotten them, he chose to suppress them. My methodology obligates me to at least try to account for such likely suppression.

Lovejoy agrees with me that Equiano constructed and fashioned an African identity at least in part for rhetorical purposes, "to situate what he knew within the framework of what was known about Africa," to quote Lovejoy again. Although Lovejoy faults me for associating Benin and Igboland, as Equiano does, several sentences later he acknowledges that "the relationship with the Kingdom of Benin is in fact plausible." Lovejoy correctly points out that in my essay I do not make "clear which ethnic groups are conflated" in Equiano's account of Igboland. Possible sources in the writings of Benezet, William Smith, Thomas Astley, Michel Adanson, John Matthews, James Field Stanfield, and John Wesley, among others, are identified and discussed in my biography. Readers can judge the fairness of Lovejoy's insinuation that

I misrepresent other critics by looking at footnote 13 in my essay. The very few Igbo words Equiano mentions in his autobiography do not demonstrate fluency. In another non sequitur, Lovejoy acknowledges an alternative source for Equiano's description of Igboland: "His information has to have been derived from his own experience, whatever he learned in London from some of his own 'countrymen.'" According to Equiano's own account, of the six people he identifies as witnesses that he "could speak no language but that of Africa" when he "first arrived in England," none met him before he had already spent years in an English-speaking environment. And none attests to where he learned the language of Africa. As I have said and written on numerous occasions, we will probably never know for certain whether Equiano was born in Africa or South Carolina.

Accepting the possibility that Equiano may have fabricated his natal African identity, Burnard and Sensbach disagree with each other on the implications of that possibility. My own position on the issue is obviously much closer to Sensbach's than to Burnard's. According to Burnard, if Equiano's account of the Middle Passage is fictitious in the sense of not having happened to him personally, then historians must bid him farewell as a useable primary source. And if Equiano fabricated in this instance, Burnard argues, "it becomes harder . . . to believe him in other areas." Burnard also says that I "always give Equiano the benefit of the doubt." Mea culpa. Acknowledging that partisanship is a biographer's occupational hazard, I would also stress that in editing his writings and reconstructing his life, I have tried to be as scrupulous as possible in verifying the information he gives us. With the very notable exceptions of Equiano's baptismal record and the 1773 muster list, wherever a written record exists that would enable us to falsify his account, I have found him to be stunningly accurate and reliable. The problem, of course, is that much of what Equiano tells us, especially in the first two chapters of his autobiography, is not falsifiable by external evidence. One of Burnard's specific doubts about Equiano concerns "the provenance of his name," Gustavus Vassa, a doubt I am not sure that I understand, perhaps because the name is so extraordinary, as Burnard notes. It is a godsend to his editor and biographer. Whenever we find a late-eighteenth-century reference to a black man named Gustavus Vassa, we can be reasonably sure that the referent is the person now best known as Equiano. I have found no reason to doubt Equiano's own account of the name's provenance, in large part because *Gustavus Vassa* is the name he used in private throughout his life. Variously spelled, it appears on muster lists from 1755 to 1773, and it remained his legal name throughout his adult life, found on his marriage record and will.

If the authenticity of Equiano's account of Africa and the Middle Passage is the primary, even only, reason historians value his life and autobiography, then many historians may agree with Burnard's conclusion that we would "have to say good-bye to Equiano as a guide to that experience" if he imaginatively reconstructed his early years. But as the conversation in this forum demonstrates, the argument about whether Equiano was a native African and the implications of the answers to that question render him historically important. The rhetorical exigency of the reclamation or invention of his African identity will probably always be historically important. Furthermore, as Sensbach points out, "Whatever is not strictly 'true' in the narrative— whatever he did not actually see or do what he said he did—becomes a kind of larger Truth in its universalism." Paradoxically, Equiano's voice is so representative of the millions of fellow people of African descent who suffered the Middle Passage and its equally horrific aftermath because his own life was so atypical. Unlike those to whom he gave a voice, because of the training and education he gained during and after his years with the Royal Navy, Equiano never experienced the grinding agricultural existence endured by the vast majority of his enslaved contemporaries. As Sensbach notes, Equiano may have been "acting as a kind of oral historian, a funnel or repository for communal memory." If he had not experienced the Middle Passage himself, he could have heard detailed accounts of it from friends like Quobna Ottobah Cugoano. I agree with Sensbach that if Equiano engaged in self-fashioning, his life and *Interesting Narrative* raises "complicated questions" about the choices of identity available to diasporan Africans.

Wherever one stands on the issue of the authenticity of the first two chapters of his autobiography, Equiano retains his historical significance. As Burnard implies, his literary significance is unquestioned. Through a combination of natural ability, accident, and determination, Equiano seized every opportunity to rise from the legal status of being an object to be sold by others to become an international celebrity, the story of whose life became his own most valuable possession. Once free from enslavement, his every action reflected his repudiation of the constraints bondage had imposed on him. As if to flaunt his liberty, he traveled the world virtually at will, recognizing the sea as a bridge rather than a barrier between continents and people. His freedom gave him the chance to move socially, economically, religiously, and politically, as well as geographically. Having known what the loss of liberty entailed, once free he took as much control of his life as he could, perhaps even revising the events in it to make a profit in a just cause.

Print enabled Equiano to resurrect himself publicly from the "social death" enslavement had imposed on him and millions of others. A genius at self-representation and self-promotion, he is a major figure in the history of the book. He defied convention by writing his autobiography and then publishing, marketing, and distributing it himself. He became the first successful professional writer of African descent in the English-speaking world. By retaining the copyright to his book, he maintained control over his "round unvarnished tale," enabling him to make changes in every one of the nine editions he published of his autobiography. The motivation for his behavior may have been as much psychological as financial. Far more than other authors, the formerly enslaved Equiano was aware of the consequences of losing control over one's own physical self and legal identity. That heightened awareness may help explain why he refused to relinquish control over the verbal and visual representations of his free self. He had spent too much time and effort establishing an identity to allow anyone else to claim ownership of it.

Equiano also defied convention by marrying a white Englishwoman and making sure that his racist opponents knew that he had done so. He announced his wedding in every edition of his autobiography from 1792 on. Mentioning his marriage was probably intended to serve a larger purpose as well: "If any incident in this little work should appear uninteresting and trifling . . . I can only say . . . that almost every event of my life made an impression on my mind. . . . I early accustomed myself to look at the hand of God in the minutest occurrence, and to learn from it a lesson of morality and religion; and in this light every circumstance I have related was to me of importance." Equiano's marriage to Susanna Cullen in 1792 anticipated the commercial union Equiano advocated between Africa and Europe. Similarly, rejected in his attempts to be sent by Europeans to Africa as a missionary or diplomat, through his *Interesting Narrative,* Equiano made himself into an African missionary and diplomat to a European audience. In the recreation of his own life, he forged a compelling story of spiritual and moral conversion to serve as a model to be imitated by his readers.

Unfortunately Equiano did not live to see the abolition of the slave trade he had done so much to accomplish. The political triumph of the abolitionist cause in 1807 came ten years too late for him to celebrate. It might not have come that soon, however, had he not contributed to the cause by so skillfully and creatively fashioning the story of his life "to put a speedy end to a traffic both cruel and unjust." He gave the abolitionist cause the African voice it needed. The role he played in the last mission of his life earned him the right to claim an African name that "signifies vicissitude, or fortunate also; one favoured, and having a loud voice and well spoken." That role also entitled him to accept the name of a European liberator of his people ironically given him in slavery. He had made himself a true "citizen of the world."

Further Readings

Africa and World History

Adeniji, Abolade. "Universal History and the Challenge of Globalization to African History." *Radical History Review* 91 (Winter 2005): 98–103.

Chakrabarty, Dipesh. *Provincializing Europe: Postcolonial Thought and Historical Difference*. Princeton, N.J.: Princeton University Press, 2000.

Gilbert, Erik, and Jonathan T. Reynolds. *Africa in World History: From Prehistory to the Present*. 2nd ed. Upper Saddle River, N.J.: Prentice Hall, 2007.

Manning, Patrick. *Navigating World History: Historians Create a Global Past*. New York: Palgrave Macmillan, 2003.

———. *World History: Global and Local Interactions*. Princeton, N.J. Markus Wiener, 2005.

McNeill, J. R., and William H. McNeill. *The Human Web: A Bird's-Eye View of World History*. New York: Norton, 2003.

Miller, Joseph C. "History and Africa/Africa and History." *American Historical Review* 104 (1999): 1–32.

Northrup, David. *Africa's Discovery of Europe, 1450–1850*. New York: Oxford University Press, 2002.

Philips, John Edwards, ed. *Writing African History*. Rochester, N.Y.: University of Rochester Press, 2005.

Stuchtey, Benedickt, and Eckhardt Fuchs, eds. *Writing World History, 1800–2000*. New York: Oxford University Press, 2003.

Thornton, John K. *Warfare in Atlantic Africa, 1500–1800*. New York: Routledge, 1999.

———. *Africa and Africans in the Formation of the Atlantic World, 1400–1680*. 2nd ed. New York: Cambridge University Press, 1998.

Atlantic History

This section is expanded from a reading list supplied by Trevor Burnard and published in *Historically Speaking* 7 (July/August 2006): 21.

Armitage, David, and Michael J. Braddick. *The British Atlantic World, 1500–1800*. New York: Palgrave Macmillan, 2002.

Bailyn, Bernard. *Atlantic History: Concept and Contours*. Cambridge, Mass.: Harvard University Press, 2005.

———. "The Challenge of Modern Historiography." *American Historical Review* 87 (1982): 1–24.

———. "The Idea of Atlantic History." *Itinerario* 20 (1996): 19–44.

Canny, Nicholas. "Writing Atlantic History; or, Reconfiguring the History of Colonial British America." *Journal of American History* 86 (1999): 1093–114.

Chaplin, Joyce. "Expansion and Exceptionalism in Early American History." *Journal of American History* 90 (2003): 1431–55.

Daniels, Christine, and Michael V. Kennedy. *Negotiated Empires: Centers and Peripheries in the Americas, 1500–1820*. New York: Routledge, 2002.

Elliott, John H. *Empires of the Atlantic World: Britain and Spain in America, 1492–1830*. New Haven, Conn.: Yale University Press, 2007.

Eltis, David. "Atlantic History in Global Perspective." *Itinerario* 23 (1999): 141–61.

Games, Alison. "History without Borders: Teaching American History in an Atlantic Context." *Indiana Magazine of History* 91 (1995): 159–78.

Gilroy, Paul. *The Black Atlantic: Modernity and Double Consciousness*. Cambridge, Mass.: Harvard University Press, 1993.

Greene, Jack P. "Beyond Power: Paradigm Subversion and Reformulation and the Re-Creation of the Early Modern Atlantic World." In *Interpreting Early America: Historiographical Essays*, 17–42. Charlottesville: University of Virginia Press, 1996.

———. "Diversity at Hopkins: Some Reminiscences. A Conversation with Jack Greene." http://web.jhu.edu/igs/Crosscurrents/Diversity_at_Hopkins.pdf (accessed February 19, 2008).

Hancock, David. "Self-Organized Complexity and the Emergence of an Atlantic Market Economy, 1651–1851." In *The Atlantic Economy during the Seventeenth and Eighteenth Centuries*, edited by Peter A. Coclanis, 30–71. Columbia: University of South Carolina Press, 2005.

Heyward, Linda, and John K. Thornton. *Central Africans, Atlantic Creoles, and the Foundation of the Americas, 1585–1660*. New York: Cambridge University Press, 2007.

Meinig, D. W. *The Shaping of America: A Geographical Perspective on 500 Years of History*. Vol. 1. New Haven, Conn.: Yale University Press, 1986.

Northrup, David. *Crosscurrents in the Black Atlantic, 1770–1965*. Boston: Bedford / St. Martin's, 2007.

O'Reilly, William. "Genealogies of Atlantic History." *Atlantic Studies* 1 (2004): 66–84.

Sensbach, Jon. *Rebecca's Revival: Creating Black Christianity in the Atlantic World*. Cambridge, Mass.: Harvard University Press, 2005.

Shils, Edward. "Centre and Periphery." In *The Logic of Personal Knowledge: Essays in Honor of Michael Polanyi*, 117–30. Glencoe, Ill.: Free Press, 1961.

Olaudah Equiano

Berlin, Ira. "From Creole to African: Atlantic Creoles and the Origins of African-American Society in Mainland North America." *William and Mary Quarterly* 33 (1996): 251–88.

Byrd, Alexander X. "Eboe, Country, Nation, and Gustavus Vassa's *Interesting Narrative.*" *William and Mary Quarterly* 63 (January 2006): 123–48.

Carretta, Vincent. *Equiano, the African: Biography of a Self-Made Man.* Athens: University of Georgia Press, 2005.

Equino, Olaubdah. *The Interesting Narrative and Other Writings,* ed. Vincent Carretta. New York: Penguin, 2003.

Eze, Katherine Faull. "Self-Encounters: Two Eighteenth-Century African Memoirs from Moravian Bethlehem." In *Crosscurrents: African Americans, Africa, and Germany in the Modern World,* edited by David McBride, LeRoy Hopkins, and C. Aisha Blackshire-Belay, 29–52. Columbia, S.C.: Camden House, 1998.

Isichei, Elizabeth. Review of *The Life of Olaudah Equiano,* ed. Paul Edwards, and *The Igbo Roots of Olaudah Equiano,* by Catherine Obianuju Acholonu. *Journal of African History* 33 (1992): 164–65.

Jones, G. I. "Olaudah Equiano of the Niger Ibo." In *Africa Remembered: Narratives by West Africans from the Era of the Slave Trade,* edited by Philip D. Curtin, 60–98. University of Wisconsin Press, 1967.

Lovejoy, Paul E. "Autobiography and Memory: Gustavus Vassa, alias Olaudah Equiano, the African." *Slavery and Abolition* 27 (2006): 317–47.

Ogude, S. E. "Facts into Fiction: Equiano's *Narrative* Reconsidered." *Research in African Literatures* 13 (1982): 30–43.

———. "No Roots Here: On the Igbo Roots of Olaudah Equiano." *Review of English and Literary Studies* 5 (1989): 1–16.

Contributors

Trevor Burnard is professor of American history at the University of Sussex. He is author of *Mastery, Tyranny, and Desire: Thomas Thistlewood and His Slaves in the Anglo-Jamaican World* (2004) and *Creole Gentlemen: The Maryland Elite, 1691–1776* (2002).

Vincent Carretta is professor of English at the University of Maryland and a senior fellow at Harvard University's W. E. B. Du Bois Institute for African and African American Research. His books include scholarly editions of the works of Equiano and of Equiano's contemporaries Ignatius Sancho, Quobna Ottobah Cugoano, and Phillis Wheatley. His award-winning *Equiano, the African: Biography of a Self-Made Man* was published in 2005.

Ricardo Duchesne is associate professor of sociology at the University of New Brunswick, Saint John, Canada. He has written several major articles on the history of Western culture and universal history.

Paul E. Lovejoy is Distinguished Research Professor at York University. He is a fellow of the Royal Society of Canada and holds the Canada Research Chair in Africa Diaspora Studies. He has authored, coauthored, edited, or coedited more than twenty books.

Patrick Manning is Andrew W. Mellon Professor of World History at the University of Pittsburgh. He is also president of the World History Network, Inc., a nonprofit corporation fostering research in world history. His recent books include *World History: Global and Local Interactions* (2005), *Migration in World History* (2004), and *Navigating World History: Historians Create a Global Past* (2003).

William H. McNeill is one of the most influential historians of our time and a seminal scholar in the field of world history. He is the Robert A. Milikan Distinguished Service Professor Emeritus of History at the University of Chicago. A past president of the American Historical Association, he is the author of many books including *The Human Web: A Bird's-Eye View of World History* (2003), written with his son, historian J. R. McNeill.

Joseph C. Miller is the T. Cary Johnson, Jr. Professor of History at the University of Virginia. He was editor of the *Journal of African History* from 1990–96 and served as the president of the American Historical Association in 1998 and the African Studies Association in 2006. *His Way of Death: Merchant Capitalism and the Angolan*

Slave Trade, 1730–1830 (1988) received several awards including the African Studies Association's Melville J. Herskovits Prize. He is currently working on a world history of slavery from the earliest human times through the nineteenth century.

DAVID NORTHRUP is professor of history at Boston College. He is a past president of the World History Association and author of several books, including *The Earth and Its Peoples: A Global History* (coauthor, 2008); *Crosscurrents in the Black Atlantic, 1770–1965* (2007); and *Africa's Discovery of Europe, 1450–1850* (2002).

JONATHAN T. REYNOLDS is associate professor of history at Northern Kentucky University. With Erik Gilbert, he wrote *Trading Tastes: Commodity and Cultural Exchange to 1750* (2006) and *Africa in World History: From Prehistory to the Present* (2008).

MICHAEL SALMAN is associate professor of history at University of California at Los Angeles. He is the author of *The Embarrassment of Slavery: Controversies over Bondage and Nationalism in the American Colonial Philippines* (2003).

JON SENSBACH is professor of history at the University of Florida. His most recent book is *Rebecca's Revival: Creating Black Christianity in the Atlantic World* (2005).

AJAY SKARIA is associate professor of history at the University of Minnesota. He is the author of *Hybrid Histories: Forests, Frontiers, and Wilderness in Western India* (1999).

JOHN K. THORNTON is professor of history and African American studies at Boston University. Among his several books is *Warfare in Atlantic Africa, 1500–1800* (1999).

DONALD A. YERXA is assistant director of the Historical Society and professor of history at Eastern Nazarene College. He has been editor of *Historically Speaking* since 2001. He is the author of three books, including *Admirals and Empire* (1991).

Index

www.ingramcontent.com/pod-product-compliance
Lightning Source LLC
Chambersburg PA
CBHW030607270326
41927CB00007B/1075